Courseware in the Classroom

Selecting, Organizing, and Using Educational Software

ANN LATHROP

BOBBY GOODSON

▲▼ **ADDISON-WESLEY PUBLISHING COMPANY**

Menlo Park, California • Reading, Massachusetts
London • Amsterdam • Don Mills, Ontario • Sydney

The sample screen shown on the cover is from the program
OREGON, copyright © MECC, and is reproduced with
permission.

This book is published by the ADDISON-WESLEY
INNOVATIVE DIVISION.
Design and cover: Richard Kharibian
ISBN-0-201-20007-4
  CDEFGH-ML-8987654

Contents

Foreword

Computers have found their way into schools faster than most of us dreamed would be possible five years ago. A PTA decides to support computer education. A parent donates a computer to the school. A teacher buys a computer for class use. By mid-1982 there was an average of two computers per school in the U.S.

What should a school do with its computers? How can it use computers most effectively to meet educational goals? What are the options? Parents, teachers, and administrators are asking these questions, fearful that, if good answers are not found, the computers may end up in the same closet with the crates of other educational technology.

Most school computers today, especially in junior high and high school, are being used to teach students about the computer itself. Computer literacy courses, programming courses, and business application courses are rapidly becoming a standard part of the curriculum. For these computer uses, all that is required is a willing, capable teacher and good textbooks. In fact, in many schools a single computer teacher can handle enough sections to give every student a one-semester hands-on course.

Other educational uses of the computer serve different purposes and make different demands on our schools. For example, computers can be used to assist with many routine teaching tasks: providing instruction, drilling facts, keeping records, diagnosing learning problems, and giving tests. A history teacher might use a computer simulation of a historical event, such as the French Revolution or a trip west on the Oregon Trail, to focus attention on the subject and to introduce a problem-solving approach to history. An English teacher may show students how to use a word-processing program as an aid to writing and revising. A math teacher could use a computer game to give students practice with the meaning of fractions.

Although little or no software is needed for teaching about the computer, instructional software is the heart and brain of these other types of computer use. The quality of the instruction depends far more upon how good the courseware is than on how good the computer is. Developing good courseware takes a great deal of creative talent and time. Schools should therefore expect to spend more money for courseware than for the computer.

It is an unfortunate fact, however, that much of the courseware currently being advertised is of very low quality. Serious classroom testing is rare. Many commercial software products lack simple user-proofing, and quite a few will not even run as advertised. Courseware reviews frequently give us the subjective reaction of the reviewer, not the results of actual use with students.

For these reasons this book is timely and important. The authors share their experience in evaluating and using courseware, building systematic collections, and recommending courseware to others. Their survey of the field gives a good picture of what is available today. If readers absorb the practical wisdom offered here they will become good consumers of courseware, and that alone will raise the standard of quality.

Arthur Luehrmann

Preface

Welcome to the exciting new world of microcomputers in the classroom! Some of you are pioneers with years of experience who are now searching for courseware to expand the curriculum you have established. We offer recommendations and guidelines to help you select the best for your purposes from among the many programs available today. You will also find suggestions for using computers in a variety of ways and in multiple subject areas.

For you who are novices we offer the assistance each of us would have welcomed several years ago. Our experiences in establishing large courseware collections for educational use may help you avoid some of the difficulties that plagued our early attempts. We encourage you to explore with your students the many creative and positive computer applications now possible.

In Section I we focus attention on the use of the computer as a dynamic aid in the teaching process. We begin with a brief discussion of WHY the microcomputer is such an important addition to the modern classroom. There is little value in establishing a courseware collection unless students and teachers are ready to use both the courseware and the hardware effectively. We do not address the use of the microcomputer in specific computer courses such as programming, but rather we emphasize the integration of the computer and appropriate courseware into all areas of the curriculum.

Section II introduces the various types of courseware that will be relevant to your objectives and to your individual learning situation. Separate chapters define general categories of courseware, using selected titles to illustrate the best qualities for each. Many of these selections reflect the combined experience of the authors and are highly subjective. Others are based on critical reviews that we regard as reliable. The goal of this section is to present samples of the best commercial courseware currently available. No attempt has been made to be all-inclusive, and the omission of a specific title should not be interpreted as a negative evaluation. Neither have we included any public domain software, as this varies greatly in quality and availability. The selection of courseware for four systems— Apple, Atari, Commodore PET, and TRS-80—reflects the reality of today's educational market. Future supplements will be expanded to include courseware for additional microcomputer systems.

Section III considers the evaluation of courseware and offers guidelines for separating that which is good from that which is poor or mediocre. The presentation of evaluation criteria and forms is followed by three sample evaluations.

Guidelines for organizing and maintaining the courseware library are developed in Section IV. The actual arrangement, location, and use of the collection will vary from one school to another. However, the Policies and Procedures Manual provides suggested patterns of organization that can be adapted to local needs.

Section V is a directory of the courseware highlighted throughout the book. Each entry and its documentation is described and identified for the machines on which it will run, the subject area in which it might be used, and the publisher. Cataloging information is included as well as sources of critical reviews of the courseware.

A few definitions will provide a common framework for our discussion. We make no claims to authority; contemporary writers are using these terms in a variety of ways. The definitions are our own and are included only for clarity.

Hardware—the actual computer equipment, including all peripherals.

Peripheral—equipment (hardware) other than the computer, such as disk drives, printers, cassette recorders, etc.

Program—a set of instructions that directs the computer to perform a logical sequence of commands in order to achieve a desired objective, written in a special computer language such as BASIC, Pascal, or PILOT.

Software—a computer program, usually stored on diskette, tape, or cartridge; the program can also be in the form of a computer paper printout called a listing.

Documentation—program support materials such as operating instructions, the program listing, and a teacher's guide that may include instructional objectives, suggested student activities, worksheets, tests, etc.

Courseware—instructional software and its accompanying documentation.

Finally, we want to remind our readers that this new field is expanding so rapidly that none of us can hope to keep informed of all new developments. We have included here the best of what we have learned from others as well as from our own explorations. Readers are encouraged to send us their recommendations of courseware to include in future supplements and to share with us their experiences in evaluating, organizing, and using the courseware collections in their own schools.

Best wishes to you and to your students in your exciting new adventures with microcomputers.

Microcomputers in the Classroom

Chapter 1

Classroom Applications

The recent surge of publicity and excitement surrounding microcomputers and their availability in the average classroom implies that computer use in the schools is a "new" activity. Actually, developmental work on instructional uses of computers began in the early 1960s. Much of this early work, in a format actually referred to as Computer Assisted Instruction (CAI), focused on the areas of math and reading. These programs utilized large banks of information and instructional materials to lead students, by a programming technique known as branching, to a level of instruction appropriate for each individual. A large mainframe computer was required for this type of instruction.

In another part of the country at that time science simulations were being developed. The best of these early programs still serve as prototypes for educational computer simulations and are now being adapted for classroom use on the microcomputer. Several far-sighted educators appeared at conferences and meetings to extol the potential educational uses of the computer. Many of their ideas are only now becoming generally accepted.

The early approaches to CAI were based upon sound educational philosophy but were sometimes lacking in creativity and imagination. The state of the art twenty years ago did not offer the graphics and sound capabilities available with today's technology. The advent of the microcomputer—smaller, portable, easily affordable, and independent of expensive phone lines and computer on-line charges—is encouraging the development of new concepts in instructional computer use.

This new technology builds on the best of the earlier research and development to offer an exciting new learning experience. Microcomputer programs that mimicked the "teletype approach" to question and answer drills are being replaced by courseware that takes advantage of the full capabilities of the new computers and display screens, using color, detailed graphics, action, and sound to good advantage.

These exciting possibilities require that even more careful thought be given to the manner in which this equipment will be used. In the days when the computer was an expensive giant, students went, one by one, to the terminal in a central lab or computer center to perform their assigned tasks. Now that the computer has been trimmed down to only a few pounds and is no longer tied by umbilical cords to a master machine, it can be moved to meet students in their normal school environments.

A single microcomputer on a cart that travels from room to room can fulfill a wide variety of classroom needs. First of all, it can provide all the teachers in an individual school with experience using a microcomputer in a classroom. This is most helpful as they begin formulating plans for integrating computers into all subject areas in the curriculum. A gradual introduction of microcomputers also encourages full utilization of the equipment. When one microcomputer is being used to its maximum capacity, the addition of a second will be welcomed. The established procedures will not need to be changed, and the program will grow easily. If, for example, five computers are given to a school without a planning and learning period, four of them might end up in a closet.

Scheduling the use of a single microcomputer, if planned in advance by the teachers who will be most involved, does not need to become a problem. The schedule should be flexible, allowing for occasional large projects and for the introduction of additional classes as interest spreads throughout the school. One plan that works well is the use of a large two-week planning and scheduling calendar on the wall of the faculty room, giving everyone an opportunity to see who is using the computer. This promotes flexibility in the schedule and equity of use without introducing rigid rules. It also encourages communication and the sharing of ideas as teachers discuss their plans and describe their experiences.

The movement and classroom setup of computer equipment can become the responsibility of a special group of students trained for the task. It might be a service club, the computer club, or even a grade or homeroom. Experience shows these groups can handle this service well and give the teachers a great deal of support, especially in the early stages of a project when they need it the most. As the school's plan for computer use evolves from these early experiences, the mechanics of equipment mobility settle into a routine unique to each school's staff, building, and student body.

The delivery of courseware to the classroom also needs to be considered. The teacher may want to have the materials in advance to look over the accompanying documentation and to prepare student material. In this case the necessary programs will be in the classroom when the computer arrives. On other occasions the student aides may bring the programs to the classroom with the computer. To avoid frustration and delay, this part of the procedure needs to be clearly defined and understood by all involved.

Connected to a large color TV, the traveling microcomputer is used as an aid to instruction for an entire class. A visitor enters a primary classroom and finds the class sitting on the floor around the computer. They are exploring with their teacher the exciting world of shapes and lines and space as they instruct the LOGO "turtle" to move across the screen. As they try out a series of instructions for the "turtle" they are, in reality, experimenting with the learning process itself.

In a junior high social studies class a simulation of a business situation is presented to illustrate the meaning of assets, profit and loss. The entire class is divided into small groups that represent competing businesses. Programs like SELL LEMONADE or MARKET* describe the developing situation, record group decisions, and respond appropriately at a single demonstration station in the front of the room. The students often learn more easily from these surprisingly true-to-life experiences than from a textbook description.

This type of computer use could be described as the demonstration model, which is especially useful when introducing new courseware to classes at any grade level. The operation of the equipment and the sequence of steps found in a particular program can be demonstrated and discussed with the entire class. When the courseware is used later by individuals or small groups of students, they will be able to concentrate on the material being presented rather than on the mechanics of the program. Younger students, new to the computer, will be especially reassured by this approach.

Ideally the setup for the demonstration model should include a large color TV positioned high enough to be seen clearly by all the students. A standard AV cart works well if it is properly balanced so it will move safely and easily from room to room. If possible, the mobile computer station should be arranged for easy use without removing the computer from the cart. In addition to the computer and disk drive there should be a small monitor for the operator, because the large screen, set for class viewing, may not be easily visible from the computer.

The mobile microcomputer station can also be set up as part of a learning center for individuals or small groups. This computer learning center should be placed where it does not distract the class but will be clearly within the teacher's view. Situated properly, it should take very little of the teacher's time to supervise the computer activity. If necessary, the computer can be moved to a table of the proper height for the students. It is important that the arrangement provide adequate room for books and papers beside the computer so students can work easily. If the large TV is still connected, it should not even be turned on while small groups are using the computer in the learning center.

The learning center model requires more computer time in any given classroom to insure sufficient working time for all student groups. However, once the operation of the equipment and the format of the program in use are understood, this activity can continue concurrently with other lessons. The ability to move

*Programs mentioned in the text are described in the Courseware Directory (Section V).

from the demonstration model to the learning center model within the classroom makes the mobile computer station particularly effective. This works especially well when the computer is first introduced into the school because it gives all students access to the computer in a relatively short time.

As a follow-up to the classroom use of a simulation it is often effective to move the microcomputer away from the front of the room, changing the demonstration model into a learning center model. Small groups of students can then go to the learning center and repeat the simulation, trying new strategies and developing their own decision-making skills. Supplementary materials can often be developed to encourage students in these explorations and to record their efforts for discussion at a later time.

Programs dealing with logic and problem solving skills also lend themselves well to computer learning centers, because much of the learning takes place as a result of student interaction. Three students seem to make an ideal working group at the computer. One student working alone may concentrate too hard on the computer rather than on the processes involved, and two students are apt to take turns "working at the computer." Three students will often watch each other and discuss the process, developing their communication and social skills as well as their thinking and reasoning skills. These types of interactive exercises enrich the usual classroom environment.

The individual student station provides a means to introduce an individual to new concepts with tutorial programs, to use the computer for remediation, to explore creative activities such as writing original computer programs, to reinforce basic skills, or to enjoy computer time as a reward for good performance or behavior. These are all valid uses of a microcomputer and require only the physical setup described for the learning center model. For these uses it may be wise to choose programs that either do not have sound or that make provision for turning the sound off; otherwise use of the computer may disturb the class. It is also important to select courseware that runs independently with little or no need for teacher intervention.

As more computers become available within the school, the learning center model can be expanded to provide individual student stations. A group of four or five microcomputers can be set up in a special room as a minilab, or single microcomputers can still be kept as mobile demonstration and learning stations providing more frequent or longer periods of use. Mobile stations appear to be preferable to the minilab in most situations, because they eliminate the need to supervise a separate location. This model also continues to promote the integration of the computer into the regular classroom activities.

One or more microcomputers can effectively be placed in a library media center where they will be available throughout the school day. Students can work individually or in small groups with programs from their classroom or from the library media center collection. Courseware thus becomes an additional form of media selected to meet students' instructional and recreational needs. The use of the computer as an additional research tool should be explored in this setting.

Equipping one microcomputer with a modem adds the capability of accessing large data bases at remote sites and is an option worth considering. This computer will give students the opportunity to check complete indexes when searching for specific material or to locate a specific reference not available in the local library. They can also access on-line news services to obtain current information on many topics.

Several microcomputers may be installed in a lab setting—a minilab of three to five microcomputers to a full lab of twelve or more—to be used as a learning center. When careful thought is given to the physical setup of this type of center, a minimum amount of supervision is needed. For instance, if the computer stations are placed around the edge of the room with all of the screens visible from a central teacher station, student activities are easily monitored by the teacher or an aide. Learning stations in any lab should provide ample room for equipment and for working with the necessary books, papers, etc.

The management of courseware in this type of study center is of prime importance. Any material brought into the lab from another classroom should have all tapes, diskettes, and books clearly marked so that they can be kept together as a unit and returned to the proper location. All courseware kept in the computer learning center should be indexed and shelved for easy access. A simple checkout system should be instituted to insure that students are responsible for the material they are using at the individual learning stations. Several suggested procedures for courseware management are outlined in Section IV.

Computer labs designed for group instruction in either programming or supplemental work in other subject areas can have an arrangement similar to the learning center. These labs can also be configured as a more traditional lecture hall with all students facing the front of the room as they work. Installing rows of computer stations parallel to the front of the room in this manner makes large group instruction easier, but the instructor can only observe student work by walking around to each individual station.

The possibility of using a network or central disk-sharing system should be considered for the computer lab. This system may use several standard disk drives at the teacher station or utilize a hard disk drive. There are advantages and disadvantages to each type of disk storage, and they should be carefully evaluated to meet the needs in a specific setting. The shared disk system makes it possible to load the same material into several learning stations or makes a variety of programs available to any student on demand. CLASSROOM MONITOR, used with one of the central disk systems, also allows the instructor to observe individual student displays on the screen at the central station, and transfer any one student's work to all screens for class discussion.

In a center equipped with a network or a central disk-sharing system it is possible to supervise access to the courseware collection from the teacher's station. However, many courseware packages now utilize copy protection schemes that prevent the use of their programs on a hard disk. Other packages incorporate procedures within the programs that may prohibit their use on a shared disk

Top left   A computer on a mobile cart can meet many classroom needs.

Top right   Individual learning stations in the library or classroom can be used by students throughout the day.

Bottom   A mini lab can be used for group instruction or individual projects.

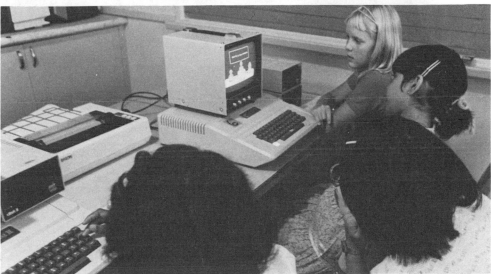

In a lab setting students work on individual assignments, as a group or
with guidance from the teacher.

Top Computers have a place in the media center.

Center The lab is the setting for problem solving assignments.

Bottom In the classroom the computer serves to demonstrate new concepts or provide material for discussion.

Daily Financial Report	- Day 2	
Stand	1	2
Glasses Made	25	50
Signs Made	1	2
Price	.10	.08
Glasses Sold	20	28
Income	2.00	2.24
Expenses	1.15	2.30
Profit	.85	-.06
Assets	4.40	4.29

Press RETURN to continue.

The computer can be the center of class discussion as students explore the world of business using THE MARKET PLACE.

system. These problems make it essential that such systems be evaluated carefully in the light of local curriculum needs and the courseware to be used before any final choice is made.

A great deal of controversy currently surrounds the entire issue of copy protection schemes, programs for use on a hard disk, and the availability of back-up copies of courseware. It is essential to have back-up copies of diskettes, which are then stored in a safe place in case a problem arises with the diskette being used. The most careful teacher or best disciplined student may accidently damage a tape or diskette, and a power surge or faulty disk drive can cause a problem without anyone realizing it. It is just as frustrating to find an excellent piece of courseware and discover that due to the copy protection scheme you cannot make a back-up copy and it cannot be transferred to a hard disk.

The other side of the controversy is equally understandable. Quality courseware is difficult, time-consuming, and expensive to develop and distribute. Each time an illegal copy is made of such a program the return on the developer's investment is cut. A compromise must be reached that will allow schools to use the best courseware and protect their purchases while at the same time guaranteeing the developers a fair return on their development costs. Schools must be allowed to secure archival copies of all software but must never use copies in any way that deprives the developer of the sale of an additional package. When this issue has been resolved we will have removed a major barrier to the continuing expansion of the use of computers in education.

Teachers and administrators who pioneer instructional applications also find the microcomputer useful for classroom management, record keeping, word processing, and the development of new material. It is really "frosting on the cake" to find that this marvelous multipurpose device still has more to offer after the students have left! Thus the computer also has a place in the faculty workroom or at home with the teacher for a weekend or vacation.

This wonderful array of new and creative educational applications exists today for you in your classroom. The equipment to accomplish all these tasks is readily available at prices that make it a realistic goal for any school. But equipment alone is not enough. The true magic depends upon a well-written, carefully selected set of instructions—the program—that activates the machine and unleashes its power for your use.

Chapter 2

Curriculum Objectives

We have found a place for the computer in the school and are now ready to find its place in the curriculum. At the secondary and college level we all too often set the computers aside in a special niche labeled computer science, math, or business education, and in this way we say to all other disciplines: "Don't bother about computers." This exclusive attitude delays the introduction of computers into other subject areas and deprives students of many creative applications in language arts, science, social studies, and the fine arts.

It is in the elementary grades that the real versatility and potential of the computer is being explored today. The wide variety of courseware now available encourages the utilization of the computer to meet many existing curriculum objectives. Computers find a place in every subject area, just as they are being integrated into every aspect of our everyday world. Given the proper courseware a creative teacher can use the computer to enrich and extend many classroom activities. This involves a choice of instructional style as well as subject area, because the intended use will determine whether a drill, tutorial, simulation, or other program is most appropriate.

Let's explore the possibilities, starting in the primary grades where attention spans are short and the use of varied approaches to learning is often the key to reaching young students. The computer is a motivating force as well as a learning tool and can be very helpful with many early developmental skills. However, letter recognition and some reading ability are necessary for operating many programs, and careful selection is especially critical at this level. HODGE PODGE and NINE GAMES FOR PRESCHOOLERS provide a nice variety of entertaining

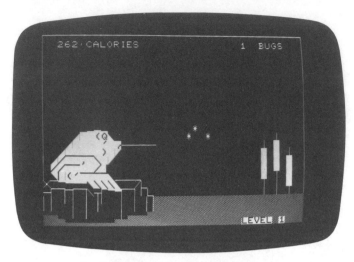

Feeding FROG is fun for young students.

activities while keeping tasks at a reasonable level for younger students, seldom requiring more than the selection of a single letter on the keyboard. CATERPIL-LAR and LETTERS & NUMBERS can help with letter recognition and with the sequencing of alphabet letters. FROG! introduces numbers in a very creative way as soon as a child is able to see the relationship between the keystroke and the graphic animation.

The computer really comes into its own at the primary level as a device for examining learning itself. Students use the computer language LOGO to explore space by manipulating lines and shapes, and thus they experience the joy of true discovery long before they are introduced to formal geometry. LOGO helps children bridge the gap from concrete to abstract, developing the ability to verbalize and express their ideas in a logical manner. With the Turtle Graphics that are a part of LOGO the child uses imagination to teach the computer to produce patterns and procedures, learning the necessity of using precise instructions and logical thought patterns. Turtle Graphics are also found in two other computer languages, Atari PILOT and Apple Pascal.

In the upper elementary grades and in the secondary schools the computer can fill many roles and accomplish a variety of tasks. We must carefully consider the actual capabilities of the computer and relate these to the curriculum in each subject area in a creative manner. The search for relevant courseware becomes much easier when the applications are well planned in advance and chosen to meet specific needs.

Because the computer is, in reality, an information machine, we will begin with an examination of its use in Language Arts. Many applications within this area take advantage of the computer's ability to supply good repetitive drill. ALPHABETIZE uses a timed game format for practice in putting words into alphabetical order, encouraging students to compete with their own best times. Grammar, parts of speech, and rules of punctuation all lend themselves well to the format of computerized drill. Such programs are especially helpful if they provide a review of basic rules and examples of correct usage, as in PUNCTUA-TION SKILLS. Spelling drill presented in the old favorite Hangman game can lead to individual discoveries of basic spelling rules that seemed meaningless or irrelevant until the student found a need for them in a competitive situation. A mad-lib game can make practice with parts of speech more interesting than the usual paper and pencil drill.

Composition on the computer offers other exciting new opportunities. The use of SCREEN PRO 40, a simplified screen editing program for very young students, allows students to concentrate on true creative writing skills rather than being frustrated by the ordeal of manually writing, editing, and rewriting. Older students can use one of the less complex standard word processing programs for creative writing, reports, and other compositions. Teachers can edit papers, and students can then make corrections with ease, giving their full attention to the changes rather than to the tedious task of copying. When the corrections are finished, a command to the computer starts the printer, and the completed assignment is ready in a matter of minutes.

The computer can generate "story starters" or samples of poetry in a particular pattern to serve as takeoff points for creative writing assignments. SAMMY, THE SEA SERPENT lets primary students participate in the story. With COMPU-POEM the student and the computer cooperate in writing original poems that may later be modified and expanded by the student.

The role of the microcomputer in reading instruction is only now being extensively explored. There are some programs designed to develop specific reading

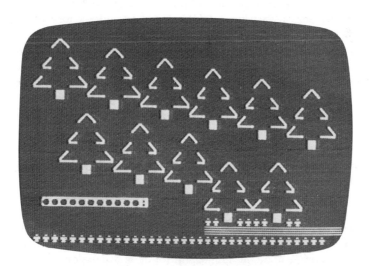

SAMMY, THE SEA SERPENT explores the forest.

APPLE PRESENTS APPLE gives a step by step introduction to the computer.

skills, speed, or certain types of comprehension, but curriculum packages that span a wide range of ages and reading abilities are not yet available. A great deal of care will have to be taken in the evaluation and implementation of these programs to be sure they are educationally sound.

The lack of keyboard skills does not seem to be a major problem for young students as long as the tasks are kept to a manageable size. In the primary grades the students are expected to enter single letters or numbers and then short words. ALPHAKEY is a simple introduction to the keyboard that also gives practice in letter recognition. Short sentences and finally paragraphs are reasonable tasks in the middle grades. It may be helpful to have an introductory typing tutorial program like TOUCH TYPING available for students who express an interest in developing these skills before reaching a grade where typing classes are offered. APPLE PRESENTS APPLE, written to introduce the keyboard and the computer, may also help students who are meeting the computer for the first time.

One of the more exciting uses of the computer allows us to bring new experiences into the classroom through simulations of many kinds. Historical simulations bring realism and a sense of true understanding to social studies in ways that are not possible with standard textbooks and films. They can be used in conjunction with any period of history, bringing the student in as a participant. Good examples are VOYAGEUR, FUR TRADER, and FURS, where the students become explorers of the trails and waterways in a new country. Simulations can be used to provide a basis for a better understanding of the modern world in which the students live. THREE MILE ISLAND and SCRAM give students an opportunity to deal with—or cause—nuclear crises. Their experiences with this type of simulation can be the foundation for class discussions, debates, related reading, and research.

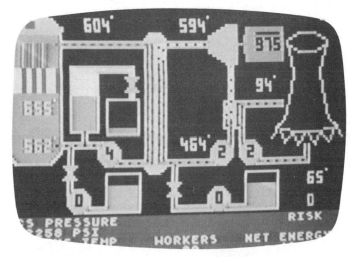

The potential danger of a meltdown is simulated in SCRAM.

This introduction of computer simulations into social studies classes also presents opportunities to develop decision-making skills. The path followed by a well-written simulation will change at each step depending upon student responses. This simulation then becomes an open-ended activity, repeated over and over, as students try new ideas and observe new results. GEOGRAPHY SEARCH gives the students an opportunity to be sailors aboard the ships searching for the New World, making them responsible for navigation, record keeping, provisioning, and other decisions that bring success or disaster.

Current affairs can be given new immediacy by classroom access to on-line news agencies through *The Source* and *Compu-Serve*. These information resources will provide many opportunities to use the computer as a source of material for discussion and as a vehicle for the delivery of ideas and experiences as they happen.

In science the computer comes into its own as a demonstration device to simulate events that might otherwise be too expensive, dangerous, or difficult to bring into the classroom. As an example, the Haber process is not easy to demonstrate to students in a conventional school laboratory. But with the program HABER, students can not only follow the process but also study the effects on the results of varying conditions.

The lack of equipment or teacher expertise that often limits science activities may be compensated for by the use of computers. Programs such as BASIC ELECTRICITY both instruct and give students an opportunity to experiment with the flow of electricity before they sit down with wires and batteries. Interactive representations of activities in the biological sciences can be introduced where they might not otherwise be available, as in TAG and the other ecology studies from ECOLOGY SIMULATIONS 1 & 2.

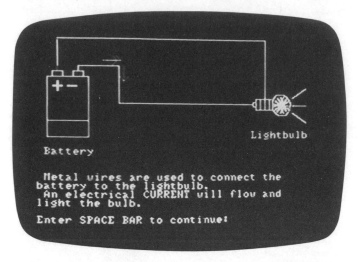

Current flow is controlled by students in BASIC ELECTRICITY.

Many mathematical concepts can be explored and illustrated at the computer. BUMBLE PLOT introduces graphing at an elementary level, and, for advanced students, PLOT illustrates a sufficient number of graphs of equations and functions to allow them to generalize the concept being presented. DARTS and CROSSBOW use a game format to reinforce the concept of equivalent fractions and the use of a number line in estimating fractions. The computer can foster a better grasp of many basic math ideas by freeing students from the demands of

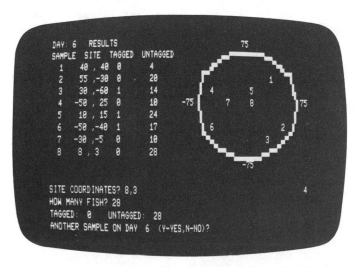

TAG lets students experiment with sampling techniques in a fish pond.

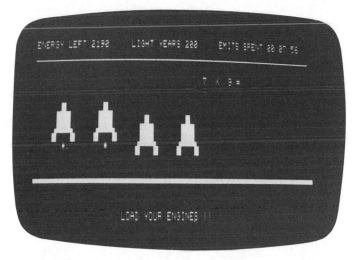

The engines are fueled with correct answers in GALAXY MATH FACTS.

computation and the likelihood that numerical errors may interfere with their understanding of the concepts involved.

Math drill and practice programs designed as total curriculum packages, such as K-8 MATH, can provide remediation, drill, and extension activities for students. Short, single concept drills can also be very effective in the classroom as part of an individual lesson and are available for a wide variety of math topics at all grade levels. FACTORING WHOLE NUMBERS, for example, offers not only drill but also enrichment activities within the given content area. GALAXY MATH FACTS generates game-formatted drills on basic number facts at any skill level. Algebra students can practice solving equations in the motivational form of an ALGEBRA BILLIARDS game, a program that adjusts the level of difficulty automatically in response to student performance.

The power of the microcomputer can also be utilized in many of the fine arts. PAINT opens the world of graphic art to young students. The use of a graphics tablet or a program like MICRO*PAINTER can introduce a whole new creative media. Although RATRUN, INTERNA-MAZE, and AMAZING were written as games, they can be used in an art class as dynamic examples of the use of perspective. INTERVAL MANIA, MUSIC THEORY, MUSIC: TERMS & NOTATIONS, and MUSIC! provide an opportunity for individual students at many levels of musical ability to explore music theory without needing access to any musical instrument.

Business education classes use the computer as a business tool, and with programs like NUMERIC DATA ENTRY and MICROCOMPUTER KEY-BOARDING it becomes an instructional device as well. DIET provides home economics classes with an opportunity to experiment with the effects of diet changes in relation to individual characteristics.

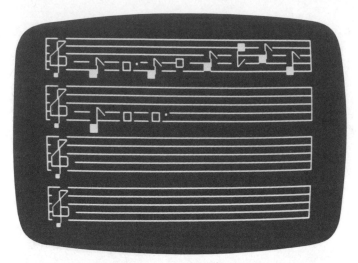

Students create their own melodies with MUSIC!

Foreign language drill can be individualized and made more interesting by adapting many language arts programs to provide practice with the vocabulary of the language being studied. SPANISH HANGMAN and PRACTICANDO ESPAÑOL CON LA MANZANA II let students proceed at their own pace and provide the challenging drill they need to develop fluency.

Some programs being incorporated into the curriculum may be short stand-alone activities, relatively limited in scope and directed toward a single objective. Other packages may be integrated series of related and/or sequential programs built around common objectives. Such curriculum packages are generally developed for a specific subject area, treat one or more specific skills, and are geared to a stated grade level or levels. They may also have an added module designed to provide teacher support and classroom management.

The choices of courseware are as wide as the imagination of the teachers and programmers involved in this new field. Programs now span all areas of the curriculum and range in instructional mode from standard drill and practice exercises, many written in game format, to challenging activities designed to develop logical thinking and problem-solving skills. This entire gamut of instructional courseware is available for use by the creative teacher.

SECTION II

Using Courseware in the Classroom

Chapter 3

Reinforcement and Remediation

The traditional mode—the historical context—within which the student has interacted with the computer has been in its role in remediation and reinforcement. The drill and practice, question and answer approach to educational programming is the most readily available format, and it also exhibits the greatest range of quality of material and presentation style. Programs of this type can be used in a wide variety of situations for several different purposes. The well-developed drill program is patient and can be tailored to meet the individual needs of each student. It is generous with its use of positive feedback and is nonjudgmental in response to errors.

Programs that provide short drill on a single concept are especially effective with younger students. CLOCK allows students to adjust the hands on a clock to match the time presented on a digital watch. CALENDAR SKILLS deals with concepts such as yesterday and tomorrow. MY TELEPHONE gives students necessary practice on their own phone number, and in the same program they have the opportunity to practice number recognition and sequencing. ALPHABET provides similar practice with letter sequences. Single concept drills can be used to check older students' comprehension of basic facts, such as their ability to name the capital of each of the fifty states in GEOGRAPHY EXPLORER USA.

Single-concept drill programs also do a good job of providing practice on specific math skills, as the computer can generate an unlimited number of examples fitting any given parameters at any desired level of difficulty. In DIVISION

Time sequences are introduced in CALENDAR SKILLS.

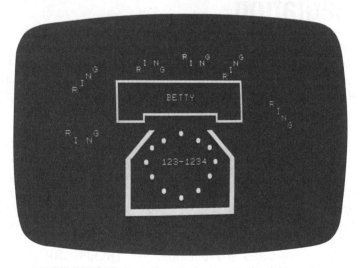

MY TELEPHONE rings when students enter the right number.

SKILLS students are able to specify the number of examples and the speed at which they want to work on any given day. FRACTIONS and GEOMETRY AND MEASUREMENT are examples of similar math drills for older students.

A series of single concept drills can be developed around one specific topic, as in FUNDAMENTAL PUNCTUATION PRACTICE. Typing skills are developed by TYPING TUTOR's drill on particular letter combinations and phrases. A more comprehensive program, such as ADDITION—ALL LEVELS /SUB-

TRACTION—ALL LEVELS, can provide remediation in a wider variety of skill areas, because it presents a continuum of problems of increasing difficulty or complexity.

Drill programs can be incorporated into a more comprehensive courseware package that includes a management module. MATHEMATICS EDU-DISKS provides practice on each elementary math operation, from introduction to mastery, and provide help for the student who has difficulty with any particular type of problem. ESSENTIAL MATH provides similar practice for secondary students. In each of these the teacher remains in control, determining the specific objectives to be addressed, the number of examples to be done at each level, and the mastery and failure level for each student. As the student demonstrates mastery of each objective, the program automatically advances to the next level, until all of the assigned topics have been covered.

There are basic qualities that should be present in any drill program for it to be truly effective. First and foremost, it must run smoothly and be error free. (It would seem that this should not even have to be mentioned as a desirable quality, but experience shows us otherwise!) Instructions for running the program should be written in a clear and concise manner and should be well formatted on the screen. These instructions should be limited to exactly what the student needs to know in order to run the program successfully. Lengthy explanations and justifications for the manner in which the program operates should be placed in the documentation rather than on the screen. The program should operate in a simple manner, always clearly indicating the student's options, so that attention is given to the subject matter rather than to the computer operation.

The best drill and practice programs make use of many of the computer's unique capabilities. One of the functions the computer performs well is generating

Initial sounds are heard and illustrated in PHONICS.

FOR SUBTRACTION, BOBBY, YOU MUST
ADD THE OPPOSITE OF THE SECOND NUMBER.

FOLLOW THESE TWO STEPS:

1. WRITE THE PROBLEM AS AN ADDITION
   PROBLEM.

2. CHANGE THE SECOND NUMBER TO ITS
   OPPOSITE.

WRITE THE PROBLEM AS AN ADDITION
PROBLEM NOW, BY PRESSING THE + SIGN.

-8 - -18 =
-8 ▉

Careful explanations in NUMBER LINE help students develop
understanding of adding and subtracting integers.

and handling random numbers or statements, allowing computer responses to students to be varied and interesting without detracting from concentration on the subject at hand. The ability to generate unlimited numerical examples and to randomly select words and sentences creates variety and holds the student's interest. THE MATH MACHINE not only generates all the necessary math problems at any given level but also provides game rewards when the student reaches the mastery level specified by the teacher.

obbalpyr

?

?r?b??ly

Player 36   Demon 24

Correct letters are left on the screen as clues in MAGIC SPELLS.

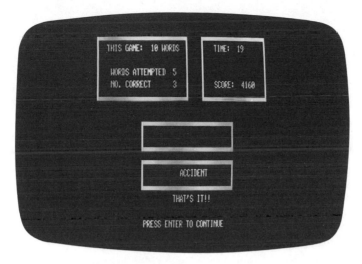

Students try to beat their own best scores in SPELL-N-TIME.

Graphics and color can be used most effectively, as in JUGGLES' RAIN-BOW, where the evolving colors and patterns provide both direction and reward. Used with care, sound can be a reward (as in DARTS) or it can be an integral and necessary part of the program (as in PHONICS). The SPELLING PACKAGE combines sound from a tape recorder with words on the screen to create a new approach to testing.

The provision of immediate feedback is especially valuable in drill and practice programs, and careful attention needs to be given to the quality of this feedback. First, the responses to the student's answers should always be encouraging and positive. Wrong answers should be corrected immediately, erased, and the student should be directed to try again—for a limited number of attempts—or suggestions should be given to guide and correct the student's reasoning. The specific purpose and design of the program will determine which option to use. Some drill programs, like HOMONYMS IN CONTEXT, keep track of student errors and present the same examples again later in the drill until the student has mastered that particular concept. NUMBER LINE immediately stops and explains the correct procedure after the student's second incorrect attempt.

If the student does not spell the word correctly the first time in MAGIC SPELLS, all incorrect letters are removed, leaving the correct letters on the screen as a hint. MAGIC SPELLS not only provides drill on teacher-selected word lists but also allows students to enter their own word lists into the spelling game. SENTENCE DIAGRAMMING informs the student when a mistake has been made and waits for a correction before proceeding. This program makes good use of high-resolution graphics for the diagrams and uses the editing capabilities of the computer to move the parts of the sentence around on the screen. In MATH SEQUENCES a wrong answer flashes on the screen and the student is encouraged to try again. A second error on any given problem automatically initiates a tutorial

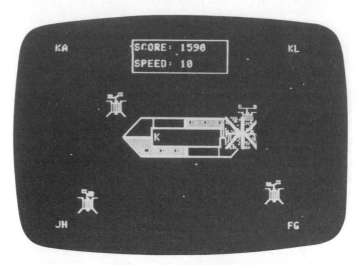

MASTERTYPE challenges students to type letter combinations fast
enough to repel the invaders.

sequence. At this point the student is guided through the correct solution of the
problem and, when ready, is presented with another similar problem to solve.
FRACTION-EQUIV 1 counters each wrong answer with a graphic representation
of the problem, and subsequent incorrect responses bring increasingly explicit
graphic explanations.

These computer-based drill programs can often be tailored to very specific
student needs rather than providing the shotgun approach to a general set of
objectives that is common in workbook drills. Modifications can occur in a variety
of ways. A simple change in style could be made, such as using multiple-choice
questions instead of those requiring that complete answers be entered from the
keyboard, which make spelling ability critical. A more subtle change could be
made within the program itself, as found in SPELL-N-TIME, where the timing
of the spelling drill automatically speeds up as the student's skill improves or
slows down in response to errors. This program also breaks words into syllables
to offer an easier task when the word is misspelled.

Closely related to drill are the educational games and game-formatted activities that utilize specific educational concepts in their design. These are often a
more interesting form of drill, taking advantage of the motivational factors inherent in game playing to encourage student participation and achievement. MAS-
TERTYPE presents all of the usual typing drills in a game format that is especially
appealing to students. The computer can also add a new twist to games already
familiar to the student. Hangman, in its many guises, is useful for spelling or
vocabulary drill when the teacher is able to insert individualized word lists.
CROSS CLUES uses a crossword format to combine spelling and vocabulary
drill with the development of logical thinking patterns. Bingo and Concentration-
type game boards, like THE LEARNING BOX, can have many applications in

language arts, social studies, and math drill. Eye-hand coordination, shape discrimination, critical thinking, and other intellectually important skills can also be developed with educational games on the computer. Game-formatted programs are most effective when the instructions are given in a manner that will relate them to the desired educational objective. They are a highly motivating and delightful supplement to the more traditional instuctional techniques.

Computerized drill and practice in their many formats offer definite advantages over the more usual form of workbook or paper-and-pencil drill. The comprehensive drill package either tests the students and places each one at an appropriate level that will be challenging without being too difficult or gives the teacher the opportunity to do so. Students receive a random selection of sentences or problems, repeating the drill only as many times as necessary to master the designated objectives. This avoids the boredom of continuing with numerous examples after the student is ready to move ahead. Wrong answers are caught immediately, which reduces the chance that incorrect procedures will be reinforced by repetition. The structure of the drill can also be varied to increase student interest, including the use of many game-formatted programs. All of these factors combine to create an individualized and highly motivating learning situation.

Chapter 4

Tutorials

One of the most promising uses of the computer is the role it can play as a tutor for the student. In this mode the computer introduces new concepts, totally new material, or extensions of previous lessons. Tutorials are usually designed for use by an individual student. Well-developed tutorials are similar in some ways to the earlier CAI programs, utilizing a programming technique known as branching by which the programmer adapts the program in progress to the student's specific needs. An incorrect or inappropriate response redirects the lesson to explain or expand a concept and then returns the student to the main program. The interactive capability and the versatile, creative displays now available on many microcomputers open up many exciting new possibilities for tutorials. Unfortunately this is one of the most difficult types of courseware to produce, but many of the programs being developed and published by CONDUIT indicate what we can expect in the future.

CO-PILOT, an interesting example of a tutorial, is designed to teach the computer language PILOT. It offers instruction in short modules, and each lesson is followed by an opportunity to practice the concept that has been presented. The computer checks each response as the student progresses and gives the option of more practice before continuing. The speed of the program is always under the student's control.

Tutorials have many potential uses. It has frequently been difficult for rural schools and smaller urban schools to offer a wide variety of courses or to institute a broad curriculum at the secondary level because of small classes and/or the lack of qualified teachers in specialized subject areas. Even in large urban schools declining enrollment has forced many advanced or less popular courses to be eliminated from the curriculum. As good tutorials become available they may meet some of the needs for special courses. However, a plan for a teacher to monitor and support students in these courses should be developed to ensure the success of such a program. Day-to-day instruction, routine quizzes, assignments, and directed study can usually be handled by the computer if the tutorial has been selected with care, but the best computer program in the world cannot replace a teacher who is available, willing to listen and discuss the issues involved.

In the elementary grades tutorial programs may eventually provide the advanced material necessary for highly motivated, curious, or gifted students. The microcomputer offers these students an avenue for independent, active exploration in areas of special interest to them. The introduction of a microcomputer and appropriate courseware into the library media center of an elementary or middle school encourages this type of independent study at an age when students are often the most curious and excited about learning.

We should also explore the possible benefits of tutorials for the student who is homebound or who must be out of the classroom for an extended period. The microcomputer can become a real link to the school for students using programs developed with their special needs in mind. Student work sent back and forth on a diskette, or better yet by a direct link to the classroom computer through a modem, can make participation in the educational process and interaction with other students and teachers possible for students otherwise deprived of such opportunities.

Tutorials will be most effective when learner objectives can be clearly defined and easily measured. The standards for successful tutorials are much more demanding than for other types of programs. To be acceptable they must take full advantage of the interactive capability of the microcomputer. Material must be presented in small increments, and the pacing must be student-controlled in a manner that does not detract from the flow of the lesson.

At every step in a good tutorial, positive feedback, presented with variety and imagination, is crucial to the student's success. In these programs the student's responses will trigger appropriate branching, and the progress through the program will be determined by the student's interaction with the material. Although branching is usually automatic it may also be available on demand when the student asks for assistance or to review the material. Frequent testing, incorporated into the program in an interesting manner, can also increase the student's feeling of accomplishment. Testing in this context is a part of the learning pattern rather than a possibly threatening evaluative tool.

Tutorials need to be carefully correlated with the existing curriculum, presenting the necessary material in an interesting manner and not simply transfering the textbook to the screen. It is important that tutorials be fully documented, self-directing, and able to provide as complete a learning situation as can be devised.

All necessary worksheets, maps, charts, reference guides, and suggested resources should be included where appropriate.

In a well-developed tutorial the student becomes involved in a very real dialog with the teacher/author, using the computer as the vehicle for communication. This technique can span the entire range of the curriculum and is one of the most exciting areas for future courseware development.

Chapter 5

Simulations and Demonstrations

Among the most creative programs being published today are those in the category of simulations and demonstrations. They can enlarge the classroom to encompass the entire world and all of recorded history. Some of these simulate historical periods that cannot be recreated authentically in the classroom. Other simulations present experiences not normally available to students, such as the

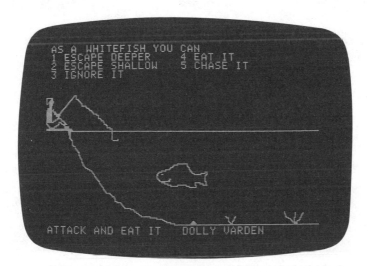

A simulation helps students learn about the food web in ODELL LAKE.

management of a presidential election campaign or the operation of a nuclear reactor. A visit, via computer, to ODELL LAKE brings the ecology of the lake into the classroom. PEST gives students an opportunity to experiment with the ecological effects of pesticides while they battle various types of infestations. Well-written simulations such as these can provide students with a sense of realism and understanding not otherwise possible in the classroom.

Simulations also provide a unique opportunity for students to develop insight and learn decision making skills with programs whose outcome will be influenced by the user's choices. In GEOGRAPHY SEARCH students actually chart their course as the ship searches for the New World. The program can be repeated, trying different options and studying the results. Well-written simulations can guide students into a discovery mode of learning not readily available in any other media. To be really useful these programs must be accurate in every possible detail; their development therefore requires much research and considerable programming skills. They are powerful teaching tools, and good ones are well worth the time it takes to locate them.

One of the most effective and widely used simulations is OREGON. This is a particularly good example because it is well written, pays great attention to historical detail, and is true to life in a surprising number of ways. It is also extremely useful in the classroom because it fits well into the standard curriculum at several grade levels. The authors of OREGON read the diaries of the original

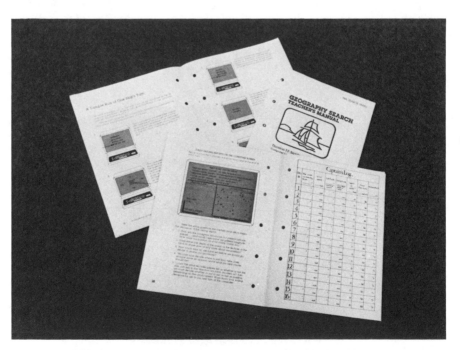

GEOGRAPHY SEARCH strategies are chronicled in the ship's log.

travelers along the Oregon Trail, figured the probability of each occurrence along the trail based on these diaries, and incorporated this information into the program. They were careful to make the program accurate both geographically and historically in order to give students a good picture of the total experience, the preparations that went into the trip, and the hardships encountered along the trail.

With careful planning OREGON can transcend the history lesson and become part of language arts and math as the students chronicle their experiences along the trail, budget their money carefully, make maps and graphs of their progress, and finally research and draw conclusions from their experiences. This is a program students will request repeatedly, trying first of all just to "make it" to the end of the trail and later to reach Oregon with sufficient money to start their new lives. They will try several strategies in planning their trip, buying their supplies, and selecting their activities along the trail. They will stop in the middle of the "trip" and ask if they must continue, suddenly seeing that they made a poor decision in purchasing their supplies or in some other component. If they can explain why they feel it was a bad decision and what the better alternative would have been, the program can be stopped and restarted and the new plan put to the test.

In simulations it is important that the program move along smoothly and as rapidly as possible to heighten student interest and excitement. The inclusion of sound and graphics should be evaluated carefully to be sure that they add to the movement and the clarity of the program in a positive manner. For example, in one of the many available versions of OREGON excellent graphics include an accurate map of the trail; however, because the map appears in every sequence of the program it has the effect of interfering with the momentum of the trip. Had the map been made available only on demand, the effect could have been to increase rather than detract from the excitement that builds as the trip progresses.

A map guides students on their way to OREGON.

Another use of simulations is illustrated in the Search series. Here the students must be able to utilize a fairly comprehensive body of knowledge on the given subject. In GEOLOGY SEARCH the students prospect for oil. To be successful they must have a good technical vocabulary and a knowledge of rock formations and of testing procedures used in the field, and they must be able to plan the finances for the exploration and marketing of the oil. If all of this sounds too involved for the average teacher or class, be sure to look at the excellent and very necessary documentation that comes with the program. The teacher's guide and the student *Searchbook* present all of the preliminary lessons in a very usable and understandable manner. The computer component of the program will not be started until the necessary lessons have been completed and the students have sufficient knowledge to participate fully in the experience. Another unique feature built into the Search programs is the fact that they are class activities. Their successful operation depends upon group participation, the acceptance of individual responsibility for specific portions of the activity, and the effectiveness of cooperative decisions made by the group as a whole.

Demonstrations incorporate many of the same qualities of the simulations but usually involve a physical object or experience. A program like SCATTER, for example, simulates an experiment usually seen in a cloud chamber. The Millikan Oil Drop experiment is effectively simulated in the MILLIKAN EXPERIMENT. Demonstrations can thus simulate objects or events that would be too difficult, too dangerous, or too expensive to replicate in the ordinary classroom. Unfortunately, these programs are still difficult to find for microcomputers. Despite the fact that this type of demonstration is one of the more common uses of the computer in industry and engineering, few have been developed for pre-college education.

The titration process was one of the earliest computer-based simulations written at the university level. TITRATE and CHEM LAB SIMULATIONS I can now be used in high school to demonstrate the entire titration procedure prior to entering the lab. Students can experiment with pressure and temperature of gases without danger in IDEAL GAS LAWS. Used in this way, demonstrations have been found to clarify the experience for the students and help to eliminate costly and dangerous errors.

A demonstration program that makes use of animated computer graphics, with the motion controlled from the computer keyboard or game paddles, becomes a new and unique teaching tool. ENGINE simulates an operating internal combustion engine and, with the student controlling the action, clarifies the interaction of the piston and valves as no still picture, film, or verbal description could. A program with a graphic representation of a beating heart circulating blood through the heart and lungs, again under student control, can enhance the student's understanding in a very special way.

Demonstrations can also provide a strong new component to the math program, as beginning "mathematicians" often miss the broad and more interesting view of mathematics in their struggle to "get the right answer." When demonstrating a basic concept, such as measures of central tendency in statistics or

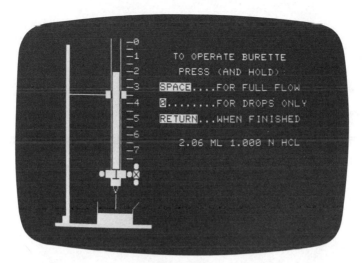

TITRATE allows students to control the chemical balance.

slope and intercept in algebra, the computer can do the simple arithmetic while the students concentrate on the concept being illustrated. FUNCTION GRAPHER gives the students an opportunity to "draw" graphs for a variety of functions easily and accurately, getting a real sense of their form and shape. In this way they can see, perhaps for the first time, the pattern and the form—and they can be exposed to the real beauty of mathematics at an earlier age.

Really good demonstrations and simulations are still hard to find but the interest and insight these programs bring to the classroom make the search worth the effort. Their use is limited only by our imagination and, for the present, by the availability of courseware.

Chapter 6

Approaches to Problem Solving

Our skill in solving problems is dependent upon our ability to analyze a situation, gather pertinent information, formulate a plan, test the hypothesis, and then generalize from whatever results are obtained. The overall goal of education should be to help students develop these techniques and apply them to many different types of problems. Such problem-solving skills usually develop slowly as a person matures, faces problems, and learns from them. Today the computer can introduce a situation, accept student responses, and modify the situation accordingly, and then it can present a solution or outcome to provide a vehicle for helping students develop problem-solving skills in an exciting and realistic manner. By carefully defining the skills we expect students to learn in this area at any given age and then searching critically through the courseware available for that age group, we can often locate good problem-solving lessons.

Many simulations can be used in this context by leading students into situations that require active problem solving. HAMMURABI, SUMER, and KINGDOM are often used to simulate various forms of government in a social studies class. They are somewhat ineffective if made available to students only as a one-time nondirected game activity. If, however, the students are challenged to find the best solution or to identify, through experiment and logic, the various constants that determine success or failure, this type of program can become a stimulating ongoing activity.

Excellent problem-solving exercises are often built into game-formatted drill and practice programs. For instance, SNARK builds on students' abilities to use a grid to locate a given point. It challenges the students to apply their basic

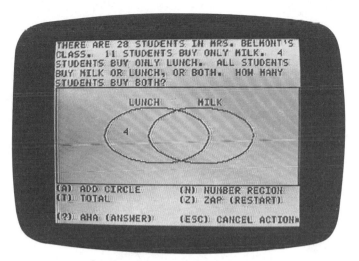

Venn diagrams are one of the strategies presented in PROBLEM SOLVING EDU-DISKS.

understanding of circles and the concept of intersecting circles to locate the elusive Snark on a grid.

Whole series of programs are specifically designed to develop problem-solving abilities. The PROBLEM-SOLVING EDU-DISKS help students develop the ability to analyze a given problem and experiment with a variety of standard problem-solving techniques, such as the use of equations, tables, graphs, and charts. Games that use compass directions or coordinate number pairs will often provide more meaningful drill than any number of math or research problems. For example, in LINEAR SEARCH GAMES and BUMBLE GAMES, the concept of using number pairs to identify a point is developed through a sequence of games, carefully reinforcing the use of rows and columns, until even a very young student can begin to understand the concept of a mathematical array. BUMBLE PLOT helps the student build on skills already developed and adds the use of positive and negative numbers to the series of plotting games.

Other problem-solving series are designed to introduce one skill at a time and then build toward the next level. MOPTOWN gradually develops discrimination skills as it asks the student to describe the attributes of the Moppets under increasingly complex conditions. Primary students can start by copying a single Moppet in "Make My Twin," while older students and adults are challenged to try to fit all sixteen Moppets into the array of the "Moptown Hotel." GERTRUDE'S PUZZLES, based on the familiar attribute blocks often used in the primary grades, can introduce logic puzzles to students of all ages. In addition to developing discrimination and logical thinking skills, these puzzles allow students to learn a great deal about the computer. The keyboard responses utilize standard editing procedures to move through Gertrude's world, and students also have the option

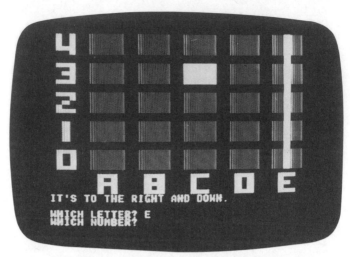

Well chosen hints add to the fun and increase student success in
BUMBLE GAMES.

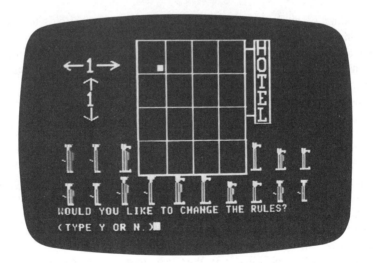

Student options in MOPTOWN add an increased dimension to the
puzzles.

to use a screen editor to change puzzle pieces or even design their own for additional challenges.

Adventure-type game programs, though usually excluded from the realm of instructional courseware, make especially effective use of the computer's capabilities. The branching techniques used traditionally in tutorials are incorporated into many of these programs to create imaginary worlds to be explored or situations to be mastered. These programs challenge students to use the same logical thought processes developed in many mathematics courses. They require analysis of a problem, development of a plan, and the logical implementation of that plan toward a successful conclusion. These are very similar to the skills students learn to apply in algebra, geometry, and higher math courses. Such programs are highly motivating, and their use as more than entertainment or reward is worth exploring.

Computer games are often used as rewards or for recreational use, but we should remember that games have traditionally been used as an enjoyable and creative approach to developing problem solving skills. Catalogs list many old favorite games, like chess and Mastermind, that have been adapted to the computer to allow students to compete against themselves, the computer, or each other. Many use the varied capabilities of the computer to present problem-solving situations that challenge the student to use imagination and creativity in finding the solution. Such games should be seriously considered when developing a problem-solving curriculum.

Problem-solving programs can intrigue students to the point where they begin to explore the whole world of programming behind the activity. Programming the computer to accomplish a given task may well be one of the most challenging problem-solving activities of all. MICRO DISCOVERY and COMPUTER DISCOVERY introduce the concepts of programming in a variety of ways within the framework of exsisting classroom activities. THE KAREL SIMULATOR and the companion book *Karel the Robot* use problem-solving techniques to introduce programming concepts and to teach the fundamentals of Pascal programming to secondary school and college students.

LOGO was devised with the philosophy of creating an open environment where a child is free to explore the process of learning, and it gives us one of the first glimpses into what we should expect from the next generation of educational courseware. Programs that put the students in control and allow them to create and expand the program as they learn will provide an interesting approach to learning and problem solving. LOGO is becoming available on many microcomputers, and manuals have been written to guide teachers in their use of these innovative new tools.

APPLE LOGO, ATARI PILOT, TRS-80 COLOR LOGO, and KIDSTUFF use Turtle Graphics to offer still another introduction to the concept of programming as a problem-solving activity. As students "instruct" the Turtle they learn to organize their thoughts, develop a plan, and try it out. Throughout this procedure they learn to verbalize abstract ideas and experiment with those ideas. These languages present interesting problem situations to students of all ages in an open-ended, creative, and interactive manner not found in other media.

A computer-based, problem-solving curriculum could be developed using the types of material discussed in this chapter. The logic programs and games should always be used wherever possible as part of a predetermined sequence of skill-building activities, taking into account the students' existing abilities at each level.

Chapter 7

Program Development Aids

As educators become increasingly aware of the capabilities of the microcomputer and become more precise in defining their courseware needs, they often look with longing at the possibility of developing their own programs. The detailed and exacting skills and the time involved in good programming mandate that for most teachers this solution is not practical. Computer-assisted program development, however, offers several alternatives.

Many programs are available that will enable the teacher to produce computer-based instructional materials without needing an extensive knowledge of programming. They range from simple, well-constructed, ready-to-use lesson frameworks to more complex, open-ended, free-form authoring systems capable of generating many types of lessons. A programming language called PILOT is also available, which was developed specifically for the use of teachers creating their own material.

The easiest to use are the relatively simple single purpose programs, designed to allow the teacher to insert instructional material on any subject. They are well documented and provide enough information to allow a teacher with little or no knowledge of programming to produce the desired lessons. QUICK QUIZ and SHELL GAMES are good examples. Both programs have menu-driven editors that lead the teacher through the entry of original textual material in true/false, matching, or multiple-choice exercises. An informational module included after each question in SHELL GAMES makes it possible for the teacher to reinforce the concepts presented.

```
*** PROBLEM ENTRY EDITOR ***
PLEASE CHOOSE FROM MENU:
1) ENTER A NEW PROBLEM
EDIT:
2) EDIT CURRENT PROBLEM: #1
3) DISPLAY CURRENT PROBLEM: #1
4) SEARCH FOR PROBLEM TO BE EDITED
5) VERIFY DATA TABLE FORMAT
6) VERIFY TABLE FORMAT TO ALLOW RENUMBER
7) END
PLEASE ENTER THE NUMBER OF YOUR CHOICE
AND PRESS THE 'RETURN' KEY
```

The SHELL GAMES menu aids teachers in designing lessons.

The motivation provided by game-formatted drill programs can be captured for any desired subject using programs like THE GAME SHOW or THE MATCH GAME. The basic format of these programs cannot be changed, but game questions, clues, and acceptable answers can be entered into the games to provide an excellent addition to traditional reinforcement activities. The instructions for adapting these programs are usually straightforward enough for both students and teachers to use them with ease.

A more complex group of programs known as authoring systems offer more flexibility and variety for program development but also require more time and effort for effective use. A variety of components may be selected and combined to form programs in many formats. Ideally the option to incorporate testing, branching, and some form of record-keeping should be available. BLOCKS 82 and CAIWARE-2D are well documented, require only minimal programming skills, and offer the capability of adding appropriate graphics to a program.

An authoring language is comprehensive and powerful in its ability to fully utilize the capability of the computer. PILOT, which stands for Programmed Inquiry, Learning Or Teaching, was devised in the late 1960s to create dialog-type material for use with college students. It was designed to allow simple text entries into the program, to accommodate a variety of student responses, and to be relatively simple for both student and teacher to use. The ease with which PILOT can be understood has expanded its use far beyond that first envisioned by the original authors. ATARI PILOT is an introductory programming language for children that also allows teachers to write simple interactive exercises with greater ease than is possible with BASIC. In contrast, TRS-80 MICROPILOT and APPLE PILOT are designed specifically for the creation of instructional

Teachers use the text editor to enter their own words and clues into the GAME SHOW.

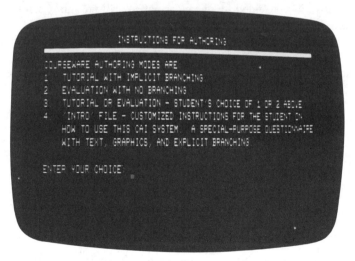

The variety of options in CAIWARE-2D make program development easier.

material. CO-PILOT is an excellent example of a tutorial that will give an interested teacher an introduction to APPLE PILOT and enough knowledge to begin experimenting with some of the programming techniques used in this language. PILOT has the potential of becoming the vehicle that will provide some excellent new software in the future, but it requires more study than the simpler programs mentioned above. It is not a method the average teacher will use to produce material for "tomorrow's lesson"!

A variety of aids for the development of computer-based material should have an important place in any courseware collection, because they currently provide the most viable methods for teachers to develop original and lesson-specific software. Learning to use the more complex authoring systems and languages is not a trivial task but is well worth the effort involved. These programs would be appropriate topics for teacher workshops, and material for a given curricular area could be developed as a group project. Programs created in this manner, evaluated and modified as necessary, could be a rich and important addition to the instructional resources in the school.

Chapter 8

Tools for Teachers

The software packages usually identified as teacher utilities include gradebook programs, curriculum management modules, test and exercise generators, and statistics programs. This wide variety of programs now being developed will help teachers produce instructional support materials and handle many routine tasks associated with teaching. Most include good descriptive manuals to help the novice.

Curriculum materials may often be generated by using a special module supplied within the instructional program. PARTS OF SPEECH allows the teacher to create tests to accompany the computer drill material, whereas COMPUTER DRILL AND INSTRUCTION provides the opportunity to generate additional worksheets to supplement the work being done at the computer.

CROSSWORD MAGIC creates crossword puzzles on the screen and on paper using words and clues supplied by the teacher or by students. WORD PUZZLE, SEARCH, and AMAZING fit words horizontally, vertically, or diagonally into an array of letters, with the size of the array determined by the user. These word puzzles can be used to provide vocabulary drills or enrichment in any subject area. Students can also create their own puzzles to share with each other.

The READABILITY ANALYSIS PROGRAM checks the difficulty level of printed materials and supplies an analysis of the sample passage. READING LEVEL provides a similar analysis and will arrange words into alphabetical word lists, lists in order of word length, or lists according to the number of syllables in each word. These programs can also be used to analyze students' compositions to determine the approximate grade level of their writing.

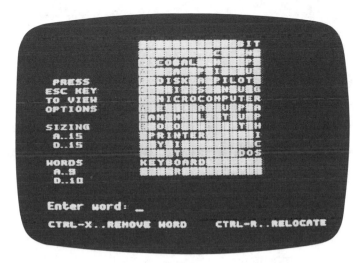

Students and teachers enjoy creating puzzles with CROSSWORD MAGIC.

Classroom management programs that use the computer's ability to administer and grade tests, keep records, analyze errors, and print reports always seem to be the answer to a teacher's dream. They may well be, but they must be selected carefully to fit your specific needs. The management modules that are part of curriculum packages vary greatly both in what they offer and in their ease of use. The MATHEMATICS EDU-DISKS management component, for example, leads the teacher through the assignment process, even presenting each objective on the screen if desired. MATH SEQUENCES includes a management module on each skill disk, making it especially useful in a lab with multiple computers. COMPUTER DRILL AND INSTRUCTION places all the management routines on special disks which is simpler for the teacher but becomes very difficult to manage when several students are using the programs simultaneously.

Management components are often built into student instructional packages, and a well-designed, carefully selected reporting module can be a great help in preparing required reports of student progress. When evaluating these programs consider your own teaching style as well as any physical constraints, such as computer availability, that might affect your ability to use the program successfully. Good management programs are fairly complex from a programming standpoint and are frequently hard to modify to meet individual needs.

Another type of management program is being developed by several publishers of elementary textbook series. Such programs are designed to support the record-keeping techniques suggested for each particular series and may vary from simple "gradebook" programs to complex objective-tracking systems. Some companies are also providing drill or enrichment material as part of a complete computer support package. As schools evaluate new textbook series it is becom-

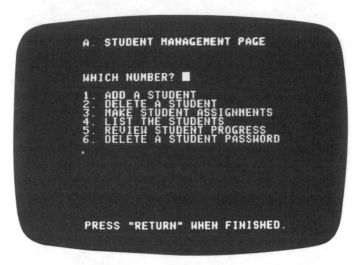

```
A. STUDENT MANAGEMENT PAGE


WHICH NUMBER? ■
1: ADD A STUDENT
2: DELETE A STUDENT
3: MAKE STUDENT ASSIGNMENTS
4: LIST THE STUDENTS
5: REVIEW STUDENT PROGRESS
6: DELETE A STUDENT PASSWORD
•




PRESS "RETURN" WHEN FINISHED.
```

The menu simplifies the process of updating student records on
MATH SEQUENCES.

ing increasingly important to look carefully at the total computer support package that accompanies each series or to question the absence of such material.

Gradebook programs now available for all microcomputers enable a teacher to keep all the usual records on a floppy disk rather than in a notebook. Some print out student reports, class rosters, etc. The benefits of computerizing a gradebook must be carefully evaluated to determine whether they are worth the time and effort required to set up and maintain the electronic record keeping system. To make these systems truly valuable the teacher must have sufficient, convenient access to a computer at all times. It is essential to evaluate gradebook programs personally and, if possible, to talk to someone using a particular program before making the purchase.

In addition to the programs written specifically for educators, several general-purpose "off-the-shelf" programs are available that should not be ignored. Word processing and data management programs can be very helpful to the teacher who will take the time to learn to use them. They have widely varying capabilities, and great care should be taken in their selection.

A good word processing program will, in effect, turn the microcomputer into a combination typewriter and filing cabinet. These programs are available for all popular microcomputers and can be used to generate instructional material and to keep it up to date and filed for immediate recall. Class lists, lesson plans, tests, and worksheets written with the word processor can be changed, corrected, and updated easily; stored on disks, they are always ready to use. Reading lists are especially well suited to storage on a word processing diskette. New books and magazine articles can be added and obsolete entries dropped without the tedious chore of retying the entire list. Quick corrections on the screen, a command to the printer, and your new classroom worksheet or bibiliography is ready. These word processing programs come with many options and in a wide price range. More complex programs are, of course, more difficult to learn to use, are usually more expensive and may include options the teacher does not need. Careful evaluation is necessary, balancing ease of use, needed options, and price as guidelines for purchase.

Data management programs, usually called Data Base Managers, will enable a teacher or administrator to keep many types of records in an easily retrievable format. Student records, inventories, and resource and reference files can be accessed and searched, and the desired information can be extracted in a matter of seconds. Because the programs vary greatly in their ease of operation and in the clarity of their documentation, these factors should be primary considerations in their selection.

As the computer takes on the additional role of teacher support through the implementation of good utility programs, teachers will find that the computer is able to handle many routine, time-consuming tasks. Computer use will give teachers more time to teach and to concentrate their efforts on students.

Courseware Evaluation

Chapter 9

The Search for Good Courseware

How do we identify the truly outstanding programs from among the hundreds currently being offered for sale to schools? What criteria do we use to separate those few that are excellent from among the many that are only satisfactory, and how do we eliminate the mediocre? Only when we select high-quality courseware that utilizes the full potential of the computer will these new tools become effective additions to our curriculum. A few schools have teachers and students who are programmers and can develop the programs they need, but most of us must search through publishers' catalogs and study critical reviews to locate courseware that will help us meet our objectives. We must then preview and evaluate each package before purchase to select for our students only those programs that represent the best expenditure of the limited funds available.

We do not need to become computer programmers nor must we be specialists in the field of computer science. We bring to the task our years of experience in evaluating instructional materials—textbooks, workbooks, films, library books, filmstrips, and other audiovisual media. We also bring our practical experience in working with students and a knowledge of their special needs. We are now ready to learn to use the evaluation guidelines and forms that will help us to recognize the characteristics of outstanding computer courseware.

Critical reviews are an excellent source of information and assistance in our search for quality courseware. The MicroSIFT reviews are the product of a national courseware evaluation project and are based on a carefully field-tested evaluation procedure. Minnesota and North Carolina have well-established reviewing projects, and other states are initiating similar activities. Several courseware review journals have recently begun to be published and are contributing to the growing collection of reliable critical reviews. Educational computing journals usually include dependable courseware reviews in each issue, and an increasing number of education journals are also publishing good review columns. The major school library review journals have also entered the courseware review field. Appendix C of this book lists these journals and other review sources with addresses and ordering information.

Critical reviews are not to be confused with the product announcements often published in journals. It is important to remember that such announcements are usually based on information provided to the journal by the publisher or even reprinted directly from the publisher's advertisement. These product announcements are useful in alerting us to new courseware that we may want to preview, especially if the package is from a publisher whose programs we have already purchased and used successfully. In other cases the publisher may be one whose programs we have rejected, but if the new program seems well suited to our needs it is often worth previewing; instructional programming is improving dramatically, and many publishers are reacting to the more sophisticated market by producing more carefully designed and educationally sound courseware.

The best reviews are usually written by an educator with experience in the subject area and with computers. They will include information on field-testing the courseware with students as well as a summary of the reviewer's opinion, and they will identify the reviewer by name, school location, subject area, grade level, etc. Each review must be read within the context of this information. A program that is highly recommended for fourth grade math might well receive a poor review from a second grade teacher who found the content to be too difficult. Experienced readers will develop a feeling for the reviews published in various journals and will learn which ones seem to be the most reliable. Even the most carefully written reviews are always to some extent subjective and can best be used as guidelines in selecting courseware for preview.

A primary consideration in selecting courseware for preview is a simple one: "Does it run on my equipment?" You are fortunate if you are still in the planning stage, searching first for the courseware to meet your instructional objectives and then purchasing the hardware required to run that courseware. You are entering the field of computer education in a carefully planned and well-organized manner. If, on the other hand, the decision in favor of a particular hardware system and a specific model of that system has already been made, you must search for courseware that will run on your system.

It is essential that you know the exact configuration of the hardware at your school. A program written for the TRS-80 will not run on an Apple unless the publisher has developed two versions and advertises the program for both systems. Similarly, PET software cannot be transported to the Atari. Conversion of courseware from one computer to another is a very complex task, especially if there are graphics in the program. Often a program written for one computer model will not run on another model manufactured by the same firm. Thus, many programs for the TRS-80 Color Computer will not run on either the TRS-80 Model I or Model III computer. A program written in Apple Integer BASIC will not run on the Apple II Plus computer unless you buy a special added language card. You will also have to determine whether your system has the correct DOS (Disk Operating System) and if it has enough memory to run the software; a 48K program will not run on a 16K machine. Programs sold only on a disk cannot be used if your system has a cassette recorder but no disk drive. Some programs require a printer or other peripheral devices. All of these factors must be checked carefully when you select courseware to evaluate.

The next problem is obtaining a copy of the program for evaluation. Many firms are understandably reluctant to provide preview copies. Courseware can be copied with relative ease, and publishers fear that some teachers might copy a program and then return it as "unsuitable." Diskettes are easily damaged, and it is difficult to determine who is responsible for replacing a damaged preview copy. You are fortunate if you live near a large microcomputer demonstration center or a computer store that offers a wide selection of courseware, or in an area where salespersons are available to demonstrate courseware for you. Another approach is to order from one of the distributors or publishers that will send courseware on thirty-day approval with a purchase order. You then have the opportunity to use the program with your students. Other possibilities are to visit a school near you where the courseware is being used, to purchase and evaluate one segment of a large courseware package, or to order one of the demonstration diskettes that many publishers are making available at a reasonable charge.

One innovative preview technique being used in some areas is that of a Courseware Fair or Preview Day. A county or larger region will schedule a preview day and invite a number of firms to demonstrate their courseware. Teachers can preview materials from several publishers and for a variety of subjects and grade levels. Preview sessions can also be planned for state and national conferences. Both of these offer the special advantage of allowing potential buyers to compare similar programs from several publishers before deciding which courseware to purchase. In schools where the hardware selection has not been made, such preview sessions are especially useful in providing additional data upon which to base the hardware decision.

Once you have located a preview copy, what guidelines should you follow? How do you decide whether you really want to purchase a particular instructional package? First, be sure to check that the program you are considering is available in a version that is compatible with your equipment, as outlined above. Second, determine whether the program really has a potential usefulness in your school. Does it fit into your curriculum? Will it meet either the general needs of many students or the special needs of some smaller group of students? An excellent program can be a waste of money if it has no application to local instructional objectives. It is much easier to make good software decisions if an overall plan for computer use has been developed and priorities of needs have been established.

When these questions are answered in the affirmative we can assume that you have located a program worth the time involved in a thorough evaluation. You have determined that it is both compatible with your microcomputer system and appropriate to your students' interests and ability levels. The next step is the establishment of useful evaluation criteria.

Chapter 10

Evaluation Criteria

The current "state of the art" of instructional programming has advanced dramatically over the past few years. The creative possibilities of the computer are being seriously explored by the best instructional designers and programmers. We are no longer pleased merely because a program will load and run without error. Technical excellence is widespread today, and anything less must be rejected as unacceptable. It is our responsibility to demand excellence in the courseware we select for our students and to convince the publishers that adequate programs are no longer good enough.

Unfortunately, much of the courseware still being sold appears trivial in terms of this potential. Some programs are little more than workbook pages transposed to the computer screen. This may be a legitimate use of the computer, especially if the program is well designed, highly interactive, and provides immediate positive feedback. In too many cases, however, the program consists of page after page of straight text, broken perhaps by occasional multiple-choice questions. The text is frequently difficult to read on the computer screen and would be more appropriately left in a book. Until students can have unlimited access to computers it is imperative that classroom activities be structured to provide the most effective use of the available computer equipment. There is little value in introducing a computer into the classroom only to deliver material in much the same way that it is already being presented in a textbook. Use your own judgment and knowledge of your students' interests and abilities in deciding whether the program you are considering is indeed worth both the purchase price and the cost of using the computer.

In evaluating a program the first question must still be, "Does it run on my computer?" The next question usually should be, "Does this program use our equipment to meet specific curriculum needs and objectives in a creative manner that represents a good investment of instructional funds and computer time?" This important issue is frequently ignored in evaluating courseware. The amount of hardware is usually limited, and the use of that hardware for a program of minimal value is difficult to justify. It is, however, important to note here that the appropriate use of a computer varies greatly from one classroom to another and is often determined by the student population and/or the instructional objectives of the school rather than by the actual design or content of a specific program.

Having established that the program does in fact run on your equipment, seems to meet one or more specific instructional objectives, and is an appropriate use of the computer within your school environment, it is time to begin a systematic review. No one evaluation form contains all of the evaluative criteria listed below. They are discussed here in detail to afford each reviewer the opportunity to identify those that seem most important and relevant to a specific situation.

CREATIVITY

Creative programs present the usual material in unusual ways and often involve the student in experiences not otherwise available. Many concepts can be explored in more exciting ways than always having students respond with "right" or "wrong" answers. Whenever possible the programs should be open ended, allowing the user to control the instructional content and to select the method of presentation. Such creative use of the computer is one of the most important factors to consider in evaluating courseware.

1. Does the program present information or instructional activities in a way not easily duplicated with textbooks, workbooks, films, or other traditional classroom materials?

2. Does the interaction between the student and the program truly involve the student in the learning process in a significant manner?

3. Are options for student control included in the program in creative ways that increase the interest and effectiveness of the lesson?

4. Can students control the learning process in terms of the number of items, level of difficulty, speed of presentation, and other factors related to the presentation of the material?

5. Are these options for student control also under teacher control and thus adjustable to the needs of various groups of students? Students in special education classes, for example, may have difficulty handling too many options, and it should be possible to limit these appropriately.

INSTRUCTIONAL OBJECTIVES

Good courseware will include clearly defined instructional objectives and suggested activities for using the package to achieve them. The objectives should be part of the written documentation, usually in the teacher's manual. They may also be stated in the program for the student. The lack of well-developed objectives may be sufficient reason to reject courseware being evaluated.

It is usually better to select a program with only a few very specific objectives, focused on one topic that is fairly limited in scope. Such a program can often present a concept or provide practice that is directly relevant to an individual student's needs or to the instructional goal being addressed. Teachers may also be more inclined to use specific, single-concept programs as part of the classroom learning activities.

Large-scale curriculum packages, such as a K-8 math sequence, should be broken down into smaller segments for evaluation, again with very specific and limited objectives for each segment. Otherwise the program may be so general that students have no clear concept of what is required or of what the desired outcome may be. Under these circumstances any learning that does take place may be either random or accidental or both.

1. Does the program documentation have well-defined objectives and goals that clearly state curricular areas and/or expected learnings?

2. Are the objectives clear to the student and perceived as relevant to instructional goals?

3. Are the objectives important to the instructor and/or to the student?

4. Does the program focus on a very specific and limited topic or objective?

5. In the case of a large instructional package, is the program appropriately divided into smaller segments?

6. Are the objectives based on sound educational philosophy, with the program designed to reflect the ways in which children learn?

7. Do the objectives make it clear whether the program is designed for drill, teaching, demonstration, testing and placement, or for some other purpose?

8. Does the program achieve its stated objectives?

CONTENT

Usually we can assume that textbooks and student workbooks are free of both factual errors and errors in grammar or spelling. Unfortunately, this was not true of much of the early software. It is still necessary to review carefully the factual content of each program for accuracy. Also check the instructional content of the program for relevance to the curriculum and to determine whether it is appropriate at the grade level(s) for which it is being considered.

1. Does the content fit well into the local school curriculum at the grade level(s) for which it is intended?

2. Does the program have instructional value and/or other valid objectives for the students who will be using it?

3. Does this presentation of the material seem to be an effective use of the computer?

4. Is all informational content factually correct?

5. Is all informational content current and not likely to become dated by slang phrases or poorly selected examples?

6. Are all graphs, charts, or other visuals included in the program well designed and technically accurate?

7. In the case of a large instructional package, does each segment stand alone in presenting all of the information needed, or is it necessary to refer to earlier segments? Are the individual segments presented in a logical sequence?

8. Is the content appropriate to the interests and abilities of students at this grade level?

9. Is the vocabulary level compatible with the reading level of the intended student users?

10. Can the difficulty level of the material be adjusted by the student and/or the teacher as necessary for effective use of the program?

11. Can word lists, problems, or other informational data be modified by the teacher, and by the student when this is appropriate?

12. Is the content compatible with other instructional materials in the school in both educational philosophy and teaching style?

13. Is the presentation logical and well organized?

14. Is there internal consistency in the design of the program, in the ways in which information is presented, and in the responses students are requested to make?

15. Is the program self-contained and free of any need for added equipment, books, or other materials? If not, are these other materials clearly specified and either included with the program or readily available in most school environments?

16. Is the content free of stereotypes or negative comments regarding race, sex, religion, age, and ethnic background?

17. Does the design of the program avoid excessive competition and violence, especially in instructional games whose goal is to shoot, kill, or destroy?

SCREEN FORMATTING

The old teletype programs scrolled information onto the screen, printing one line at a time in a continuous roll. This should be avoided by presenting one screen, or page, of information at a time. Students should be able to control the screen by advancing or returning to any desired page at will. Special attention must be paid to avoiding the frustration of having a page advance before the user has finished reading it, and avoiding the opposite frustration of spending long extra seconds in front of the screen waiting for a program to continue.

1. Is each separate screen neat and uncluttered?
2. Is the amount of information displayed at one time appropriate rather than confusing?
3. Is there a limited number of choices at any given time and is there a clear indication of the desired response?
4. Can the user access specific pages, advancing or returning to earlier material as desired?
5. Does the user control the timing of screen advancement?
6. Are spelling, punctuation, and grammar correct in each screen display?
7. Are maps, graphs, or other illustrations clear and simple to interpret?
8. Are all graphics displayed effectively?
9. Is color used effectively on systems that offer this option?

INSTRUCTIONS

Good instructions make a program easier to use and therefore more attractive to the student. They also make it less difficult for the teacher to integrate the program into other classroom activities.

1. Are instructions available within the program itself, appearing on the screen as needed and not requiring that the user refer to the written documentation?
2. Are there instructions in the documentation as needed to further explain the structure and operation of the program?
3. Are the instructions clear, complete, concise, and well formatted on the screen?
4. Do the instructions assume that the user is naive, avoiding computer jargon and explaining computer operations as needed?

   Statements such as "Syntax error, redo from start" or "Break in line 230" can be confusing or discouraging to the user and are clearly unacceptable. On the other hand, "Please wait—Loading from disk" would be helpful.

5. Will the student be able to operate the program independently after reading the instructions, or will teacher assistance be needed?

6. Does the user have the option of by passing the instructions?

7. Can the user return to the instructions if needed during the program (HELP)?

8. Are there instructions for ending the program (ESCAPE) if the user wants to stop?

9. Is there a MENU or other control to allow the user to access any desired segment of the program rather than always having to enter at the beginning? For younger children, is there a picture menu?

10. In the event that the program "crashes," or ends unexpectedly, are there instructions for continuing rather than forcing the user to return to the beginning?

11. Are there instructions to tell the user how to control the speed and sequence of paging?

12. Can the teacher edit the instructions if desired?

13. Is the reading level of the instructions appropriate to the intended grade level of the users?

14. Does the program really work the way the instructions indicate it will?

STUDENT RESPONSE

Well-designed courseware is "user friendly," making it easy for the student to work through the program without being inhibited by the mechanics of computer operation. Clear and explicit instructions help to make this possible. It is also necessary to handle data entry routines in ways that will feel natural to the user.

1. Are data entry routines consistent and easy for the student to use?

    Programs that use "Press RETURN/ENTER" for part of the lesson and at other times accept the student response without waiting for RETURN/ENTER can be confusing and sometimes frustrating. Some poorly designed programs "crash", or end unexpectedly, due to irregularities of this type; others generate apparent student errors or advance unexpectedly to the next screen. Such faulty design is clearly unacceptable.

2. Does the program use common conventions and symbols for data entry?

    "PRESS SPACE BAR TO CONTINUE" is fairly common and easily learned by students. A good program should not complicate student responses with unnecessary choices that break the concentration properly focused on instructional content.

3. Is there a cursor or other indicator to show where the response is to go?

4. Is there an example, or do the instructions explain what response is desired?

   Programs with multiple-choice questions, for example, should provide help to the user who enters the actual answer rather than the correct letter for that answer.

5. Does the program offer help when the student response appears in an unexpected form?

   A student might enter "two" instead of 2, or "Washington" instead of "George Washington," and a well-designed program will provide appropriate help.

6. Is the student given an opportunity to correct errors before the program reacts to the entry?

7. Is the keyboard "locked" to prevent unwanted or inaccurate responses?

8. Is the amount of typing appropriate to the grade or ability level of the expected user?

9. Is the program designed to ask for only one item per RETURN/ENTER?

10. Does the user control the speed of data entry?

    Unless the program is in a mode for testing, timed drill, or game, the student should be able to take as much time as is necessary to enter a response.

11. Are there appropriate alternatives to keyboard entry, such as the use of a light pen, joysticks, or game paddles when these are easier or more fun?

    Such alternatives are especially important if the courseware is to be used with very young children or with handicapped students.

12. Finally, is the program highly interactive, providing frequent opportunities for creative responses from the user?

PROGRAM RESPONSE TO STUDENT

The variety and creativity of program responses to the student should be evaluated with special care. This potential for effective interaction between computer and student can be a major factor in discriminating between an excellent program and one that is only adequate.

1. Does the program provide positive rewards for correct responses that are more interesting and exciting than are the responses to failure?

Hangman-type programs often provide more effective graphic rewards for student failure than for success. Making it more fun to fail than to succeed is poor educational psychology, and programs that do so should be rejected.

2. Is the student prompted to make a response after a reasonable amount of time has elapsed?

3. When appropriate, does the program limit the number of incorrect responses and, except in timed drills or tests, does it provide help, hints, or the correct answer after a reasonable number of attempts?

   "Try again" may simply lead to another guess and can be discouraging to the student who is already trying very hard but doesn't understand the item. One good technique, especially with math or spelling programs, is to keep the correct part of the response on the screen and indicate where the corrections need to be made.

4. Is the user instructed to enter the correct response before continuing with the program?

5. Is the reward for success appropriately designed to motivate continued good performance while avoiding overpraising? It seems unrealistic to exclaim "EXCELLENT! YOU'RE A GENIUS!" when the correct answer is finally achieved after several attempts. Intermittent and varied rewards are usually more motivating than are those that appear in the same form in response to every correct answer.

6. Does the program branch to harder or easier material, or present items faster or slower as appropriate in response to student performance?

   Creative programs take advantage of the capability of the computer to branch, or to select from among several possible program paths, in response to the student. A correct answer may cause the program to branch to a more difficult level or to more challenging material. Errors may elicit a new approach to the item missed, help the student to discover the desired answer, or return to a previously mastered and less difficult level.

7. Is the response to errors nonjudgmental, friendly, patient, and free of insults or sarcasm?

   Programs that state, "You're wrong" or that present a frowning face, large black X, or similar response will often seem negative to the user. Even "Try again" can be discouraging unless some hint or other assistance is available.

   It is important that the symbol used for feedback be clearly understood by the user, especially if it indicates an error. A large X is generally regarded as meaning "wrong," but a check mark can be used to mean either "right" or "wrong," depending upon the teacher and the locale.

8. Are items that were answered incorrectly repeated later in the program?

9. Is it possible to get a list on the screen and/or a printout of items that were missed?

10. Do the responses avoid using computer terms that are unexplained and perhaps confusing to the user?

MOTIVATIONAL DEVICES

The wide range of motivational strategies available today represents one of the most innovative and creative aspects of using the computer for instruction. Yet it is essential that we make the realistic assessment of these motivational devices an important part of our evaluation. Many are very effective, whereas others may be showy but have little or no instructional value. In some cases they may actually distract the student or impede the flow of the program. We cannot assume that programs are automatically improved by the addition of color, graphics, or other "bells and whistles."

1. GRAPHICS FOR INSTRUCTION should use illustrations as valuable additions to the program, helping to achieve the objectives by demonstrating, explaining, or otherwise clarifying the material. Graphics used merely for the sake of having graphics in a program are often ineffective, distracting, or boring.

   Different microcomputers have widely differing graphics capabilities, and when programs are rewritten to run on several different systems it is important that the graphics be redesigned to take full advantage of each computer. Do not assume that unusually good graphics on one system will necessarily be as good if the same program is offered on another computer.

2. GRAPHIC REWARDS should be clever, presented in a random sequence, appropriate to the age and interest level of the user, and fast and varied enough to maintain interest after several uses of the program. If the same graphic appears after every correct response, the cumulative effect is often boring or irritating. Graphics that take a relatively long time to load from the disk and then remain on the screen for several seconds independent of student control can also be boring. They frequently lose their appeal after several runs through the program, especially if the same design appears after every correct response or always at the same point in the program. Well-designed graphic rewards do not interrupt the continuity of the program but rather heighten the user's interest and enjoyment, holding attention even after many runs through the program.

3. RANDOM ORDER in exercises and rewards is another source of motivation that can be very effective, especially with programs that students

use repeatedly. When a specific set of questions or problems is presented in random order, the program should check that each item is presented only once, except in cases where items missed are repeated later in the program. When problems, sentences, or other materials are randomly generated, the student and/or teacher should have the option of setting difficulty levels. Programs designed to generate random sentences or stories may need some check to eliminate inappropriate items. Rewards, whether as statements or graphics, are also more interesting when presented randomly.

4. TIMING can be effective when properly used. Otherwise it can lead to user frustration by presenting material too quickly or, for the able student, far too slowly. Either extreme detracts from even the most effective presentation. In testing mode the timing factor may be preset by the teacher to meet a particular objective. For regular classroom use it is usually better to allow the student to control the timing whether the program is presenting reading material, math problems, or other information.

5. SCORING can also be either positive or negative. There is little if any psychological value in having a student receive a very low score, especially in competition with a classmate. Scoring probably should be used only when the student is working at an appropriate ability level and thus has an opportunity to score well. The most effective competition frequently occurs when the student competes with his or her own previous best score. Other activities pit the student against the computer; again, this can be either effective or discouraging, depending upon the quality and sophistication of the program in setting an appropriate difficulty level. Scoring may also be part of a testing or management program, but in this case the score is most usefully reported only to the teacher.

6. COLOR can be a powerful motivational tool and can also be used to explain and clarify informational concepts. Color is essential in some programs and a definite positive feature in many others. It can, however, be a distraction in some situations, and colored text may at times be more difficult to read than black and white. Color is more expensive, requiring a color monitor or TV, and the evaluator should determine whether it is worth the added cost. Color cannot automatically be counted as a plus in a program and should be critically evaluated for its effect on the total presentation.

Does the program have color?

Is the color used effectively?

Is the color a motivating factor in this program?

Does the color make the text difficult to read, or does its use restrict the text to a narrow window and thereby reduce the effectiveness of the written material?

Is the program more fun to use because of the color?

Is color used to make any visual explanations more understandable, or is it distracting?

7. SOUND can be either essential or supplemental in a program. It can be an effective device or a classroom nuisance, and it is sometimes both at the same time.

Does the program have sound?

Can the sound be turned off completely by the teacher or student if necessary?

Is the sound used effectively?

Is the sound used for instruction?

Is the sound used only for reward?

Is the sound used to signal a student error? In this case it may have a negative impact on the student who does not want the entire class notified that she or he has made a mistake, and it definitely should be under student control.

When music is an important part of the program, is the technical quality acceptable? If notes are being displayed, do they match the notes being played?

Can the volume of the sound be controlled?

8. GAME FORMAT may or may not be regarded as an appropriate motivational device in the field of educational computing. Some teachers are totally opposed to the concept of presenting instruction in a game format. Others enjoy games of all kinds, including the use of strictly recreational games as rewards for good classroom behavior and/or good work. The well-constructed game is highly motivating to many students, making even drill and practice programs challenging and exciting. The final decision often depends upon the philosophy of the teacher, the classroom situation, and the quality of computer games available. Many recreational games with little or no obvious instructional value provide students with a surprising amount of practice in the development of problem solving, reasoning, and critical thinking skills. Other games are excellent for improving eye-hand coordination and control of reflexes. Younger children can master many reading readiness skills and concept development lessons in the guise of game playing.

Does the game encourage the development of a positive self-image?

Does it avoid excessive competition?

Can the difficulty level be adjusted to the ability of the student so the game is challenging but not so hard that it becomes discouraging? Is the computer programmed to make these adjustments automatically, or is teacher intervention required?

Is excessive violence avoided?

Does the game have sound educational objectives that help the student to learn some new skill or information or to practice those previously introduced?

Is the game fun?

9. GAMES FOR REWARD can be used effectively in many classrooms. Some teachers allow free game time to reward students who have reached an agreed-upon instructional goal. Game time can also be used as a reward for good behavior.

   Short games are built into some programs as reward segments for successful performance. These can be brief, stand-alone games or can build sequentially in response to correct answers until a rocket is launched or some other goal is achieved.

10. PERSONALIZATION, the introduction of the student's name into the computer program, may be more effective with younger children. Some teachers are philosophically opposed to any "humanizing" of the computer and dislike the use of such pseudo-dialogs between computer and student as "Hi, Susan, I'm your friendly computer and we're going to play a game together." Others find this to be an effective and useful approach. Until there is more research in the field this issue will continue to be settled largely on the basis of instructor opinion. A good program probably should not be rejected simply because the instructor does not like personalization or because personalization is omitted. A useful option is control of personalization by students and/or teachers.

TECHNICAL QUALITY

A program should be completely reliable in normal use over a long period of time. It should be technically sound, free of programming errors, and easy to operate. Data entry techniques should be "user-proof," and under no circumstances should a student be able to "crash" or abruptly end the program by making unanticipated entries or by pressing RETURN or ENTER unexpectedly. Several years ago we may have felt that we had to accept programs with technical flaws, but this absolutely is no longer necessary; courseware that does not operate correctly should be returned to the producer with a letter outlining the problems.

DOCUMENTATION

The quality of the materials accompanying the program can add a great deal to its instructional effectiveness and should be evaluated within the context of the total package. An occasional outstanding program may be worth purchase even if you must develop your own documentation. On the other hand, excellent documentation that is attractively printed and bound in a sturdy case must not be allowed to camouflage a program that is not of top quality. The inclusion of several of the following items will definitely enhance the instructional value of most programs.

1. Teacher's guide or manual containing a statement of objectives, summary of the program, recommended grade levels, estimated student time needed for completion, suggestions for classroom use, supplemental activities, and an indication of prerequisite knowledge or skills.

2. Complete operating instructions.

3. Clearly written instructions for students, usually in the program and on paper.

4. Program listing, especially when data statements are presented in random order in the program and it is difficult to check all of them without a listing.

5. Printout of a sample run.

6. Directions for changing the data or timing.

7. Pre- and post-tests.

8. Student materials such as worksheets, maps, graphs, illustrations, and suggested activities. These student materials should be appropriate to the grade level and either available to be reproduced legally and easily, or for purchase at a reasonable price.

9. Notes on other needed equipment, materials, books, or information.

10. Bibliography of resources and added references.

11. A key to standard textbook series, indicating where the program fits into each.

TEACHER UTILITY

Quality programs are easy to use in the classroom and operate with a minimum of teacher intervention. The teacher should be able to load a program, provide simple instructions for the students, and then continue with other classroom activities while one or more students complete assigned work at the computer. Menu-driven programs will allow the same student to start over or another student to take a turn at the computer with little if any need for technical assistance from the teacher.

An increasing number of programs provide some form of classroom management capability. This may include scoring and reporting of student performance, automatic adjusting of individual difficulty levels according to parameters set by the teacher, testing students and assigning them to appropriate lessons, or the ability to individualize the program in other ways specified by the teacher. Some provision should be made to keep students from accessing any files or assignments other than their own and to lock them out of teacher management files. Summary reports and grades also should be protected from unauthorized student access. It is especially helpful if grades and detailed reports of student progress can be printed by the teacher.

Textbook lessons may also be correlated with the program and assigned to students in response to their performance. The use of any management option should be explained in some detail in the documentation and should operate as simply as possible. It is important that these management functions actually save teachers' time rather than taking longer than would be needed to complete the same task in traditional ways.

It is also important to evaluate the ease with which changes can be made in the instructional content of the program. We have noted that the inclusion of many teacher options is to be considered a definite plus in our courseware evaluation. The best programs make it simple to set difficulty levels or timing, to revise the word lists or other data, and to change the reward statements or other parameters of the program. Programs that offer a menu of teacher options and allow these changes to be made without having to enter new data statements into the program itself are definitely more "teacher-friendly" and deserve a higher rating.

1. Can the program be used by students in the classroom with relatively little need for teacher intervention?

2. Does the management system make it simple to add and delete individual student files as needed and to update records with little effort?

3. Can records and grades be printed?

4. Does the management system actually save time and effort?

5. Are there simple techniques to allow teachers to change the word lists, data statements, or other parts of the program?

SUMMARY

No one program is likely to exhibit all of the positive characteristics outlined in this chapter. They are presented here as a set of standards against which courseware can be measured. The forms discussed in Chapter 11 can be analyzed in terms of these criteria, and you can then select the form that most nearly matches your perceived needs. Additional items can be added to any one of the forms to tailor it to local needs, or an entirely new form can be devised to include only those items desired. One word of warning based on our own experience in working with teachers and evaluation forms: if you really want teacher input into the evaluation process, then keep the form as short and simple as possible. There is a fine line between creating a form that is complete in covering all aspects of the evaluation process and making the form so complex and lengthy that it discourages the very teachers it was designed to help.

Chapter 11

Evaluation Instruments

Many evaluation forms are currently available, and new ones appear regularly in the journals. Two are reproduced in Appendix B, and others are described with information on how to obtain them. Three forms are used in this chapter to illustrate the critical evaluation of specific programs.

MicroSIFT Evaluator's Guide for
Microcomputer-Based Instructional Packages

MicroSIFT is a federally funded national clearinghouse for microcomputer-based courseware evaluations and related information. It operates with a network of evaluation sites coordinated by the Computer Technology Program of the Northwest Regional Educational Laboratory in Portland, Oregon.

The MicroSIFT guide is designed to facilitate a thorough, in-depth courseware evaluation. It is well organized and highly structured with clear explanations of the evaluation criteria used. The guide has been field-tested nationwide, and this final version is both a useful tool for the reviewer and a model for identifying excellence in courseware.

ODELL LAKE has been selected for review as an example of a well-constructed simulation. It brings into the classroom an experience that is truly interactive and that could not be provided in any other way.

 **Northwest Regional Educational Laboratory**   micro SIFT

COURSEWARE DESCRIPTION

PACKAGE TITLE Odell Lake (MECC Science Vol. 3)

VERSION ___4.3___   COST $30

PRODUCER/DATE___MECC___   /   1980

SUBJECT AREA ___Science___ GRADE/ABILITY LEVEL ___4-10___

SPECIFIC TOPIC ___Biology, Food webs___

DEWEY DECIMAL/~~LIBRARY OF CONGRESS~~ # ___574.5___

SEARS SUBJECT HEADING(S) ___Biology, Ecology___

ERIC DESCRIPTORS ___Biology, Ecology___

MEDIUM OF TRANSFER: ☐ Tape Cassette   ☒ 5″ Flex. Disk
                          ☐ ROM Cartridge   ☐ 8″ Flex. Disk

REQUIRED HARDWARE:

Apple II (48K)
Single disk drive
Monitor

REQUIRED SOFTWARE:

MECC Science Vol. 3

TYPE OF PACKAGE: ☒ Single Program   ☐ Integrated program
                                                                series component

Other programs on disk are:
   Fish, Minerals, Quakes, Ursa

INSTRUCTIONAL PURPOSE: (Please check all applicable)
   ☐ **Remediation**   ☒ **Standard Instruction**   ☒ **Enrichment**

INSTRUCTIONAL TECHNIQUES: (Please check all applicable descriptions)
☐ **Drill and Practice**   ☐ **Game**   ☐ **Learning Management**
☐ **Tutorial**   ☒ **Simulation**   ☐ **Utility**
☐ **Information Retrieval** ☒ **Problem Solving** ☐ **Other**

DOCUMENTATION AVAILABLE: Circle *all* that are available in the computer program (P) or in the supplementary materials (S).

P Ⓢ Suggested grade/ability level(s)   P Ⓢ Teacher's information
P Ⓢ Instructional objectives   P S Resource/reference info.
P S Prerequisite skills or activities Ⓟ Ⓢ Student's instructions
P Ⓢ Sample program output   P Ⓢ Student worksheets
P Ⓢ Program operating instructions   P S Relationship to standard
                                                  textbooks
P S Pre-test   P Ⓢ Follow-up activities
P S Post-test   P Ⓢ Other *suggested*
                                                  classroom activities

IS LISTING AND ALTERATION OF THE COMPUTER PROGRAM ALLOWED?

no

PRODUCER'S FIELD-TEST DATA IS AVAILABLE
- ☐ ON REQUEST
- ☐ WITH THE PACKAGE
- ☐ NOT AVAILABLE

?

ESTIMATE THE EXPECTED TIME OF STUDENT INTERACTION WITH THE PACKAGE NEEDED TO ACHIEVE THE OBJECTIVES. (CAN BE STATED AS TOTAL TIME, TIME PER DAY, TIME RANGE OR OTHER INDICATOR.)

20 to 30 minutes for initial exploration of the program

INSTRUCTIONAL OBJECTIVES: ☒ Stated   ☐ Inferred

Understand concept of food webs.
Identify 1st, 2nd, + 3rd order of consumer on web.
Explain role of each animal, and indicate effects of man on lake and lake on man.
Define words related to food web.

INSTRUCTIONAL PREREQUISITES: ☐ Stated   ☒ Inferred

Assumes students have been introduced
    to food chains and webs.

Assumes knowledge of terms involved.

————————————————————————————————

**DESCRIBE PACKAGE CONTENT AND STRUCTURE (INCLUDING
RECORD-KEEPING AND REPORTING FUNCTIONS):**

This is a simulation of life in Odell Lake
using the discovery approach to learning
Students learn about food webs by
assuming the identity of each fish in the
lake and making choices about behavior.

RATING: Circle the letter abbreviation which best reflects your judgment. (Use the space following each item for comments.)

IMPORTANCE: Circle the letter which reflects your judgment of the relative importance of the item in this evaluation.

☒ Check this box if the evaluation is based partly on your observation of student use of this package.

Northwest Regional Educational Laboratory

COURSEWARE EVALUATION

PACKAGE TITLE _Odell Lake (MECC Science Vol. 3)_
REVIEWER'S NAME _Amy Johnston_
VERSION _4.3_
DATE OF REVIEW _April 1981_

RATING
SA — Strongly agree
A — Agree
D — Disagree
SD — Strongly disagree
NA— Not Applicable

IMPORTANCE
(optional)
H—Higher
L—Lower

microSIFT

	Rating					Importance		Item
CONTENT	SA	Ⓐ	D	SD	NA	Ⓗ	L	1. The content is accurate. (p. 15)
	Ⓢ	A	D	SD	NA	Ⓗ	L	2. The content has educational value. (p. 15)
	Ⓢ	A	D	SD	NA	Ⓗ	L	3. The content is free of race, ethnic, sex, and other stereotypes. (p. 16)
	Ⓢ	A	D	SD	NA	Ⓗ	L	4. The purpose of the package is well-defined. (p. 16)
	SA	Ⓐ	D	SD	NA	Ⓗ	L	5. The package achieves its defined purpose. (p. 16)
	Ⓢ	A	D	SD	NA	Ⓗ	L	6. Presentation of content is clear and logical. (p. 33)
	Ⓢ	A	D	SD	NA	Ⓗ	L	7. The level of difficulty is appropriate for the target audience. (p. 33)
	SA	Ⓐ	D	SD	NA	Ⓗ	L	8. Graphics/color/sound are used for appropriate instructional reasons. (p. 34)
INSTRUCTIONAL QUALITY	Ⓢ	A	Ⓓ	SD	NA	Ⓗ	Ⓛ	9. Use of the package is motivational. (p. 34)
	Ⓢ	A	D	SD	NA	Ⓗ	L	10. The package effectively stimulates student creativity. (p. 34)
	Ⓢ	A	D	SD	NA	Ⓗ	L	11. Feedback on student responses is effectively employed. (p. 35)
	Ⓢ	A	D	SD	NA	Ⓗ	L	12. The learner controls the rate and sequence of presentation and review. (p. 36)
	Ⓢ	A	D	SD	NA	Ⓗ	L	13. Instruction is integrated with previous student experience. (p. 36)
	Ⓢ	A	D	SD	NA	H	Ⓛ	14. Learning is generalizable to an appropriate range of situations. (p. 36)
	Ⓢ	A	D	SD	NA	Ⓗ	L	15. The user support materials are comprehensive. (p. 37)
	Ⓢ	A	D	SD	NA	Ⓗ	L	16. The user support materials are effective. (p. 38)
	Ⓢ	A	D	SD	NA	Ⓗ	L	17. Information displays are effective. (p. 38)
TECHNICAL QUALITY	Ⓢ	A	D	SD	NA	Ⓗ	L	18. Intended users can easily and independently operate the program. (p. 39)
	Ⓢ	A	D	SD	NA	Ⓗ	L	19. Teachers can easily employ the package. (p. 41)
	Ⓢ	A	D	SD	NA	Ⓗ	L	20. The program appropriately uses relevant computer capabilities. (p. 42)
	SA	Ⓐ	D	SD	NA	Ⓗ	L	21. The program is reliable in normal use. (p. 42)

22. (Check one only) (p. 43)
☐ I would use or recommend use of this package with little or no change.
☒ I would use or recommend use of this package only if certain changes were made.
   (Note suggestions for effective use under Section 25.)
☐ I would use or recommend use of this package only if certain changes were made.
   (Note recommended changes under Section 24.)
☐ I would not use or recommend use or recommend this package. (Note reasons under Section 24.)

23. Describe the major strengths of the package. (p. 43)

Students are given clear, immediate, and reinforcing feedback.

Simulation activities appropriately involve students.

24. Describe the major weaknesses of the package. (p. 44)

Vocabulary above 4th grade level.

Shape of fish doesn't vary as the name changes, making it difficult to distinguish among the different fishes, and hard to solve the problem.

The manual needs more instructions, with an answer key for all of the problems.

25. Describe the potential use of the package in classroom settings. (p. 44)

Useful as part of regular science curriculum, either with entire class or small groups in a learning center.

Could be used as enrichment for small groups or individuals, depending on the curriculum.

National Council of Teachers of Mathematics Guidelines
for Evaluating Computerized Instructional Materials

The guidelines developed by NCTM are especially helpful to the novice. A brief introduction to instructional software is provided as well as information on locating programs for review, sample evaluation forms, an explanation of the evaluation criteria, and a list of resources for additional information.

The evaluation forms are shorter and less complex than those developed by MicroSIFT. They take less of the reviewer's time to complete and also seem to require less time spent in studying the evaluation criteria. The guidelines are not math-specific and can be used effectively for any type of courseware in any subject area.

An unusually flexible drill and practice program, SPELL-N-TIME, is reviewed here using the NCTM Evaluation Checklist and Documentation Sheet.

---

1. The grade levels and ability levels for a particular program are primarily determined by the concepts involved. Other important factors are reading level, prerequisite skills, degree of student control, and intended instructional use. It is possible for a program to be flexible enough to be used across a wide range of grade levels and ability levels.

2. Some programs are designed for use by individuals. Others have been or can be modified for participation by two or three persons at a time. Simulations or demonstrations often pose opportunities for large-group interaction. A given program may be used in more than one grouping, depending on the instructor.

3. The time required for the use of a program will vary considerably. Include loading time for cassettes. A time range is the appropriate response here.

4. Instructional programs can be categorized according to their uses. Some programs may have more than one use, thus falling into more than one of the following categories:

Drill or practice: Assumes that the concept or skill has been taught previously.

Tutorial: Directs the full cycle of the instructional process; a dialogue between the student and the computer.

Simulation: Models selected, alterable aspects of an environment.

Instructional gaming: Involves random events and the pursuit of a winning strategy.

Problem solving: Uses general algorithms common to one or more problems.

Informational: Generates information (data).

5. These are factors relevant to the actual use of the program from the point of view of an instructor.

Flexibility: A program may allow the user or the instructor to adjust the program to different ability levels, degrees of difficulty, or concepts.

Intervention or assistance: A rating of "low" means considerable teacher intervention or assistance is required.

6. These are factors relevant to the actual use of the program from the point of view of a student.

Directions: The directions should be complete, readable, under the user's control (e.g., should not scroll off the screen until understood), and use appropriate examples.

Output: Program responses should be readable, understandable, and complete. If in response to student input, the output should be of an acceptable tone and consistent with the input request.

Screen formatting: The formats during a program run should not be distracting or cluttered. Labels and symbols should be meaningful within the given context.

External information: A program may require the user to have access to information other than that provided within it. This may include prerequisite content knowledge or knowledge of conventions used by the program designer as well as maps, books, models, and so on.

System errors: System errors result in the involuntary termination of the program.

Input: A program should ensure that a user knows when and in what form input is needed. It should avoid using characters with special meanings, restrict input locations to particular screen areas, and require minimal typing.

7. These are matters relevant to the subject-matter content of the program.

Focus: The program topic should be clearly defined and of a scope that permits thorough treatment.

Significance: The instructional objectives of the program must be viewed as important by the instructor. Also, the program should represent a valid use of the computer's capabilities while improving the instructional process.

Soundness or validity: The concepts and terms employed should be correct, clear, and precise. Other important factors are the rate of presentation, degree of difficulty, and internal consistency.

Compatibility: The content, terminology, teaching style, and educational philosophy of the program should be consistent with those generally encountered by the student.

9. Competition, cooperation, and values are concerns that may be a function of the way a program expresses them. (War gaming and the "hangman" format are sample issues.) Also, the "humanizing" of the computer may serve for motivation or to reduce anxiety, but it also may become tedious, misleading, and counterproductive.

The summary of student performance can be dichotomous (win or lose), statistical (time expended or percent of items correct), or subjective (as in the evaluation of a simulation). It may be for student, teacher, or both.

SOFTWARE EVALUATION CHECKLIST

PROGRAM NAME **Spell 'N' Time** SOURCE **School CourseWare Journal** COST **$12.95**
SUBJECT AREA **Language Arts** REVIEWER'S NAME **Bob Warren** DATE **9-13-81**

1. INSTRUCTIONAL RANGE
   1-12 grade level(s)
   all ability level(s)

2. INSTRUCTIONAL GROUPING FOR PROGRAM USE
   ✓ individual
   ___ small group (size ___)
   ___ large group (size ___)

3. EXECUTION TIME
   10-20 minutes (estimated) for average use

4. PROGRAM USE(S)
   ✓ drill or practice
   ___ tutorial
   ___ simulation
   ___ instructional gaming
   ___ problem solving
   ___ informational
   ___ other (_____)

5. USER ORIENTATION: INSTRUCTOR'S POINT OF VIEW

low				high	
·	·	·	·	⊙	flexibility
·	·	·	⊙	·	freedom from need to intervene or assist

6. USER ORIENTATION: STUDENT'S POINT OF VIEW

low			high		
·	·	·	⊙	·	quality of directions (clarity)
·	·	·	·	⊙	quality of output (content and tone)
·	·	·	⊙	·	quality of screen formatting
·	·	·	·	⊙	freedom from need for external information
·	·	·	·	⊙	freedom from disruption by system errors
·	·	·	⊙	·	simplicity of user input

7. CONTENT

low				high	
·	·	·	·	⊙	instructional focus
·	·	·	·	⊙	instructional significance
·	·	·	·	⊙	soundness or validity
·	·	·	·	⊙	compatibility with other materials used

8. MOTIVATION AND INSTRUCTIONAL STYLE

passive			active		
·	·	⊙	·	type of student involvement

low		high		
·	·	⊙	·	degree of student control

none	poor		good		
	·	·	⊙	·	use of game format
⊙	·	·	·	·	use of still graphics
·	·	·	⊙	·	use of animation
⊙	·	·	·	·	use of color
⊙	·	·	·	·	use of voice input and output
⊙	·	·	·	·	use of nonvoice audio
⊙	·	·	·	·	use of light pen
⊙	·	·	·	·	use of ancillary materials
·	·	·	·	·	use of _____

9. SOCIAL CHARACTERISTICS

present and negative	not present	present and positive	
		✓	competition
	✓		cooperation
	✓		humanizing of computer
	✓		moral issues or value judgments
	✓		summary of student performance

Reprinted with permission from: GUIDELINES FOR EVALUATING COMPUTERIZED INSTRUCTIONAL MATERIALS
National Council of Teachers of Mathematics $3.75
1906 Association Dr. Reston VA 22091

GENERAL DESCRIPTION OF THE PROGRAM (i.e., purpose of the program)

Timed drill in spelling words as they flash onto the screen
and then disappear. Speed and accuracy produce higher
scores, with each student competing with her or his own best
score. Spelling words are entered onto the diskette or tape by
teacher (or student) and many separate lessons can be
created and saved, using the same program.

SPECIAL PROGRAM CHARACTERISTICS (e.g., use of graphics or sound, designed for use
by groups of two or more persons at a time, level of difficulty can be modified by teacher
(only) or student, exit from program is controlled by the teacher (only) or student, etc.)

Speed of word presentation is automatically adjusted to student
response, flashing each word for a shorter time after several correct
spellings and leaving the word on the screen for a longer period
after a series of errors.
Words are presented randomly from a list entered by the teacher.
Cumulative score and time are displayed on screen, encouraging
student to improve speed and accuracy.
Word is presented one syllable at a time if student mis-spells
the word twice.

DIRECTIONS FOR USE OF THE PROGRAM (e.g., directions not presented in the program
itself but needed for program execution, directions regarding the use of the program within
the total instructional process, notes regarding program options, etc.)

Instructions for student must originally be given by
teacher (type the word after it disappears from the screen)

Very clear instructions for changing the word list are
included in the written documentation.

ANCILLARY MATERIALS REQUIRED (e.g., books, worksheets, charts, data lists, dice, geo-
metric shapes, lab equipment, etc.)

Paper to copy list of mis-spelled words displayed on
screen at end of each program run.

ADDITIONAL DOCUMENTATION AVAILABLE (check box for each type)

☐ sample run (location _____)

☒ program listing (location _documentation_____)

SAMPLE SOFTWARE DOCUMENTATION SHEET

PROGRAM NAME: Spell 'N' Time

SUBJECT AREA: Language Arts

PROGRAM CLASS

✓ isolated program

____ part of a ____ program cluster

INTENDED AUDIENCE(S)

____ teachers

✓ students in grade(s) all

____ other _____

_____

PROGRAM USES: (1 = primary, 2 = secondary)

1 drill or practice

____ tutorial

____ simulation

____ instructional gaming

____ problem solving

____ informational

____ other _____

_____

CRITICAL PREREQUISITE SKILLS

Some degree of familiarity with words presented

NAME(S) OF PREREQUISITE PROGRAM(S)

_____
_____

NAME(S) OF FOLLOW-UP PROGRAM(S)

_____
_____

DATE OF THIS DOCUMENTATION

9-13-81

_____

PROGRAM SOURCE

name: School Courseware Journal

address: 4919 N. Millbrook

Suite 222B

Fresno CA 93726

phone: 209-227-4341

program cost: $12.95

SYSTEM REQUIREMENTS

computer: TRS-80

language: BASIC

memory needed: 8K bytes

input mode: ✓ cassette

✓ 5¼-inch diskette

cartridge

other _____

_____

output mode: color monitor

✓ B/W monitor

printer

plotter

other _____

_____

CLASSROOM VALIDATION (describe)

Used with 5th grade Class for individualized spelling practice

TIME FOR AVERAGE
EXECUTION   10-20 minutes

OVER ➡

Reprinted with permission from: GUIDELINES FOR EVALUATING COMPUTERIZED INSTRUCTIONAL MATERIALS
$3.75 from National Council of Teachers of Mathematics, 1906 Association Dr. Reston, VA 22091

California Library Media Consortium for Classroom
Evaluation of Microcomputer Courseware

Simplicity of use was the primary consideration in developing this form. The major portion, a Checklist of Evaluation Criteria, is designed to help the teacher look critically at various aspects of the program and indicate whether each is satisfactory. Perhaps the most important section is the brief description of the program and the questions that follow regarding student response. The form is designed to be self-explanatory, and there is no accompanying documentation.

MOPTOWN, the program reviewed on the Consortium form, represents the new generation of courseware appearing on the market. It can be used for a variety of purposes at many grade levels and illustrates the type of creative and interactive programming now being implemented so effectively on the computer.

CALIFORNIA LIBRARY
MEDIA CONSORTIUM FOR
CLASSROOM EVALUATION
OF MICROCOMPUTER COURSEWARE
1983

FOLD HERE AND STAPLE TO RETURN (ADDRESS ON REVERSE)

Program title _Moptown_

Title on package/diskette _____

Microcomputer(s) brand/model _Apple II_ Memory needed _48_ K

Language _✓_ BASIC (or _____) Version/copyright date _1981_ Cost _$50_

Publisher _Apple Computer_

Peripherals needed: _✓_ Disk drive(s) _____ Cassette _____ Printer (Other _Color TV_)

Other materials/equipment needed _____

Backup copy available? _provided with purchase_

* *

Reviewed by _Linda Benton_ Grade level/subject you teach _K-6 Computer Center Specialist_

School/District _Stevenson School / Whisman_

Address/Phone _750 San Pierre Way Mt View_

May we use your name in the published review? _Yes_

THANK YOU FOR YOUR HELP. PLEASE RETURN IMMEDIATELY TO THE ADDRESS ON THE BACK.

PROGRAM TITLE _Moptown_ SUBJECT AREA(S) _Used with both_ _math & language_

SUGGESTED GRADE LEVELS (K 1 2 3 4 5 6) 8 9 10 11 12 College Teacher use
have used personally _in 5_
TYPE OF PROGRAM (check all that apply)

__ drill/practice	✓ problem solving	__ game	__ word processing
__ simulation	__ tutorial (teaches)	__ testing	__ classroom management
__ demonstration	✓ educational game	__ utility	__ authoring system

SCOPE (check one)
✓ one or more programs on single topic   __ one program in an instructional series
__ group of unrelated programs   __ multi-disk curriculum package

EVALUATION CRITERIA

YES NO N/A

GENERAL DESIGN: ✓EXCELLENT __GOOD __WEAK __NOT ACCEPTABLE
✓ __ __ Creative, innovative, effective use of computer
✓ __ __ Well-organized curriculum design
✓ __ __ Free of programming errors
✓ __ __ Free of excessive competition or violence
✓ __ __ Free of racial, ethnic, or sex stereotypes

EASE OF USE: ✓EXCELLENT __GOOD __WEAK __NOT ACCEPTABLE
✓ __ __ Simple and complete instructions
✓ __ __ Screens are neat and attractive
✓ __ __ Speed and sequence of paging can be controlled
✓ __ __ Technically easy to operate
✓ __ __ Any sound is appropriate and can be turned off

CONTENT: ✓EXCELLENT __GOOD __WEAK __NOT ACCEPTABLE
✓ __ __ Factual material, grammar, and spelling are correct
__ __ ✓ Word lists, problems, and speed can be modified
✓ __ __ Interest level, difficulty, typing, and vocabulary are appropriate
✓ __ ✓ Provides easier or harder material in response to performance
✓ __ __ Responses to errors are helpful, avoiding sarcasm or scolding
✓ __ __ Response to student success is positive, enjoyable and appropriate
✓ __ __ Avoids clever graphics that make it "fun to fail"

MOTIVATIONAL DEVICES USED: ✓EXCELLENT __GOOD __WEAK __NOT ACCEPTABLE
__ graphics for instruction   ✓ color   ✓ game format   ✓ sound   __ timing
✓ graphics for reward   ✓ scoring   ✓ random order   __ personalization
Comments:

DOCUMENTATION AVAILABLE: __EXCELLENT __GOOD __WEAK __NOT ACCEPTABLE
__ none   ✓ instructions appear on screen
✓ instruction manual   ✓ suggested classroom activities
✓ teacher's guide   ✓ instructional objectives
✓ student worksheets   __ workbook   __ tests
Comments:
Manual has many group Moptown activities using
Moptown attributes. Computer games reinforce these.

OVERALL OPINION ** OVERALL OPINION ** OVERALL OPINION
✓ ____ Great program! I recommend it highly!
____ Pretty good/useful. Consider purchase.
____ OK, but you might wait for a better one.
____ Select only if suggested modifications are made.
____ Not useful. I don't recommend purchase.

INSTRUCTIONAL CONTENT AND OBJECTIVES

- What are the objectives of the program and how does it achieve them?

  To develop logic and language concepts — achieved by a set of colorful, attribute games, from easy to hard.

- What learning outcomes are expected?

  Students progress to the more difficult levels as they learn to recognize the attributes and to understand how they are used.

- What classroom management, testing, or performance report capability is provided and how easy is it to use? *none*

  How many students/classes can be handled by program?

  Is it possible to make backup copies of student records?

- Describe any special strengths of program.

  Colorful. Nice, gradual transition from easy to ~~hard~~ difficult. Great graphics!

- Comments/concerns/questions

  Encourages discovery learning

- Suggestions to author/publisher

BRIEFLY DESCRIBE STUDENTS & THEIR RESPONSE TO PROGRAM

Grade level/subject *K – 6*

Behavior observed that indicates learning took place *Students were able to progress to the harder levels.*

Enjoyment, boredom, or other reaction expressed *Enjoyed by all age levels in our K-6 school — many*

Any problems experienced *children wanted to play the games repeatedly.*

Any quotes you want to share

PLEASE USE ANOTHER SHEET IF YOU HAVE ADDITIONAL COMMENTS
***** THANK YOU FOR YOUR HELP*****

11/82

Other Forms

Appendix B gives reproductions of forms that can be copied and ordering information for ones sold by other publishers that should not be reproduced from this book. Select the form that seems best suited to your needs—or develop your own. In either case, remember that critical evaluation before purchase is essential to your successful use of commercial software.

Chapter 12

The Evaluation Process

It is important to make the courseware review process a cooperative effort whenever possible. You may decide to form an evaluation committee. Several teachers,
perhaps from various grade levels and/or subject areas, may review the program
together or individually. Administrators, aides, and interested parents may become
involved. At the very minimum two different teachers need to look at the program, use it with students, and share their evaluations in order to develop a fairly
reliable idea of its potential value.

Student reaction is one of the most valuable parts of the evaluation process.
This may be achieved informally by observing students as they use the program
in several classrooms, or students may be asked to complete an evaluation form
of their own. Watching students interact with the program, the computer, and
with one another frequently gives you an entirely different feel for the program
being considered. Text that seemed to be well presented in isolation may become
repetitive or dull when exposed to the reality of classroom activities. A program
that perhaps seemed to be too simple or lacking in serious content may fascinate
the students and offer hours of happy and productive practice with spelling words,
math facts, or other drill. Classroom use of a computer program should be included
in an evaluation whenever possible, preferably using it with the students for whom
it may be purchased.

At this point we will assume that you have located a program to review and
read any available critical reviews. You have established your own evaluation
criteria and either have selected a form to use or developed one of your own. An
evaluation committee is ready to begin its work.

Your next step is to obtain a preview copy by ordering from a publisher or distributor with a liberal return policy. Several now offer a thirty-day preview policy on orders accompanied by a purchase order or check. It is very important, however, that you not abuse these policies by ordering courseware you probably will not purchase or by making an illegal copy of the program and then returning it. Preview policies are just beginning to appear in the courseware market in response to our frequent requests, and it is essential that firms offering such policies feel they are being used with honesty.

Once you have received the program you are ready to begin your evaluation. Read the documentation carefully. Some teachers reject a program that has little or no documentation. An occasional gem may be worth purchasing even if you must develop your own manual and support materials, but the lack of documentation is usually a strong negative factor. On the other hand, take care that excellent documentation does not obscure the fact that the program itself is mediocre or has little relevance to your curriculum. Good documentation will state the instructional objectives, suggest classroom uses and related activities, and provide all needed instructions.

Use the documentation to check the hardware requirements against the system(s) available at your site. Note any special features or potential difficulties. Read through any student worksheets or other supplemental materials to see whether they are appropriate for your students or will need to be revised. If there is a management system, determine whether it is simple or difficult to use. A complete listing of the program is an especially valuable item to have included with the documentation, especially if the program branches to various levels or has randomly selected data statements. In these cases a listing is often the only way to explore the entire program.

Now run through the program to get a good feel for it before you use it in the classroom. Explore the purposes and objectives as well as the general content. Does it run? Is it actually compatible with your equipment? Can you understand the instructions, or, in those unfortunate cases where there are no instructions, can you operate the program anyway?

Be a "good" student and work your way through the entire program in a positive manner. Are the instructions clear, easy to follow, and written on your grade level? Try to get correct answers and perform the tasks assigned as well as possible. Are you challenged by increasingly difficult material in response to correct answers, or are you bored by having to repeat many examples at the same level even though you are performing well? Did you learn anything or feel that the program was of value to you? Would you ever want to use it again?

Now be a "poor" student and go through the program again. Miss the same question several times in a row and observe how the computer responds to errors. Hit the wrong keys as if by mistake. Hit an extra, unnecessary RETURN/ENTER key and try to "crash" the program. Deliberately misunderstand the instructions. Note whether you feel dumb or frustrated. If there is a beep or other sound that tells the whole class when you make an error, can it be turned off? Pay special attention to whether the program is helpful, or perhaps even creative, in response to your blundering attempts to use it. Does it provide additional help, give simpler explanations, or branch to easier material? As a final step in this initial review session, run through the program as if you are a very negative student. Enter irrelevant responses, often in the wrong format, to see if you can end the program abruptly. A good program will ignore all of these attempts to "crash" the system, foil your efforts to circumvent the instructions, and patiently remind you of the response requested. Could you eventually get interested in the program despite yourself and begin to work seriously?

Now complete your first evaluation form. Be sure you are checking the program against your objectives and the criteria you have established. If the criteria do not seem to cover certain aspects of the program that are important to you, it may be necessary to add one or more items to the evaluation form.

At this point you may already be totally convinced that you do not want to purchase the program, either due to technical failures, poor design, or a complete lack of relevance to your curriculum. It is still necessary to complete the review form and keep it on file to share with other teachers and to prevent your ordering the same program for preview again at a later date. You may also decide to publish the review.

To continue the evaluation process, we will assume that you do like the program and want to try it with students. You may decide to use it with the entire class, with small groups, or with individuals. Observe the students' reactions. Are they eager to finish the program? Do they want to run it again or share it with friends? Use any worksheets or other suggested classroom activities and observe students' performance. You may also ask for informal feedback or request completed evaluation forms from the students.

Complete the classroom preview and record student reactions in whatever way you have chosen, being careful not to bias their responses by your own initial opinion of the program. Students may find creative uses for the program that have not occurred to you, or the program may prove to be unexpectedly useful for groups such as special education or gifted students.

In making your final evaluation of the program remember to pay close attention to whether this courseware represents a valid and creative use of the computer. Does it meet specific objectives in your classroom? A program may be excellent but still have little value in your local situation. Next, complete the form you selected and decide whether or not to recommend purchase. If others have worked with you in the review process, this is the time to combine your observations and to reach an agreement regarding your recommendations. Remember that the quality of courseware is improving rapidly, and you may well decide to defer a purchase until you locate a program that students and teachers will use with enthusiasm.

When several classrooms, either in the same school or in different schools within the district, want to use the program it will be necessary to determine what duplication policy is available from the publisher. Can you make legal copies for use in several classrooms and/or schools? Does the publisher offer a licensing agreement that allows the school to make multiple copies, or is there a reduced price structure for additional copies? Can the program be loaded onto a networking system for use with multiple computers operated from a central station? Is there any provision for exchanging the program for an enhanced version that may be published in the future? Can you make legal back-up copies? What is the policy for replacing damaged copies of the courseware? In the case of large and expensive packages is it possible to lease the courseware on an annual basis instead of purchasing it? Finally, is the price realistic? If possible, compare several similar programs for price and duplication policies.

After the decision to purchase or not to purchase has been made, offer a critical review to one of the educational computer journals or newsletters. If you return the program, enclose a letter or copy of your review to explain your decision not to purchase. Many distributors request such customer feedback and will drop an unsatisfactory program from their catalog. If you ordered your preview copy from the original publisher, critical feedback may encourage the publisher to either withdraw or improve the program. Our refusal to purchase anything other than excellent programs for our classrooms and our willingness to publicize our critical evaluations will help to improve the courseware available. Because the quality of this courseware has a great impact on the success with which we use computers in our classrooms, the time and effort spent in locating, evaluating, and selecting excellent courseware is indeed a worthwhile investment.

The Courseware Library

Chapter 13

Organizing the Collection

The microcomputer courseware collection will vary in organization from site to site just as it varies in content. The content is determined by the curriculum and instructional objectives of the school or other site. The organization of the collection depends upon who the users will be and where the collection is located.

In this chapter we will consider three locations for the courseware collection: in the classroom or computer lab, in the library media center, and in the professional library or display center. Our suggestions for each of these three situations can serve as guidelines to develop a pattern of organization suitable to your own local needs.

There is always a trial-and-error period as we learn to handle any new media. When audio-visual materials first appeared in our school library media centers, we approached their use in a variety of ways. Students had access to some materials, whereas others were limited to teacher use only. Some items were kept permanently in the library media center or classroom, and others could be checked out for use at home. We are following the same path of experimentation today as we integrate microcomputer courseware into existing media collections or set up new and separate courseware libraries.

Decisions regarding circulation routines, back-up policies, shelving arrangements, and whether to list the courseware in a book catalog, on catalog cards, or to have direct on-line access to the collection via computer will all be determined by who and where the users will be. An attempt must be made to balance both student and teacher requests against the need to protect the collection. Policy decisions should be made only after the patterns of expected usage and the needs of the users have been surveyed. One caution to keep in mind is that the collection will probably grow far beyond current projections, and any system must be easily expandable.

COURSEWARE IN THE CLASSROOM OR COMPUTER LAB

Alphabetical order by the *title* of the diskette or tape is a fairly straightforward arrangement that works well with the relatively small collection usually found in a computer lab or classroom. Both students and teachers can easily locate the specific program they want.

There are occasional problems with title arrangement when several popular programs are on the same diskette or tape. Users will probably look for ORE-GON, for example, rather than for the diskette title, MECC ELEMENTARY

```
MECC Elementary Volume 6

Furs
Nomad
Oregon
Sumer
Voyageur
```

```
Oregon

    on MECC Elementary Volume 6
```

Sample diskette title and program title cards for an alphabetical title file.

VOLUME 6. A decision must be made whether to use the diskette or tape title instead of an individual program title. One solution is an alphabetical arrangement by diskette or tape title combined with a card index file of all individual program titles. The index file of program titles would indicate the diskette/tape title.

The primary disadvantage of an alphabetical title arrangement is that it is difficult to group together all of the programs on any particular subject. Subject access can be provided by adding subject cards to the title card index or developing a separate subject index.

The use of courseware in a classroom or computer lab is usually closely supervised by a teacher or an aide, and it may not be necessary to keep a written record of the students or teachers using each program. In a large lab or in situations where courseware is taken from the lab or classroom it may be necessary to set up some system to check out the programs. The various circulation options discussed in Chapter 14 can be adapted for use in the classroom or lab as needed.

Many computer labs will use some form of disk-sharing system. In these labs the courseware is often stored in a file drawer or cabinet that is not accessible to students, and the actual handling of the diskettes or tapes may be restricted to the teacher or other person in charge. Student worksheets or related materials can be issued by the same person. Arrangement by title in this situation is simple and usually requires no special indexing other than that provided on the network system.

Several good database management programs are currently available that can be used to maintain a courseware inventory record. They can also be used to search the collection and to print selected title or subject lists if desired.

```
OREGON TRAIL

    Oregon, on MECC Elementary Volume 6
```

Sample subject card for OREGON on MECC Elementary Volume 6.

COURSEWARE IN THE LIBRARY MEDIA CENTER

The introduction of microcomputers and courseware into our library media centers presents new challenges as well as new opportunities. Library media specialists will decide whether to catalog the courseware as part of the total collection or to establish a separate courseware library, perhaps arranged alphabetically by title or numerically by Dewey Decimal number, identification number or accession number.

The Dewey Decimal Classification is probably the most appropriate system of classification to use when the courseware is to be cataloged. Programs can then be integrated into the collection according to a system already being used for other media and one with which students and teachers are familiar. Complete sets of catalog cards can be prepared and filed in the card catalog in the library media center, or the information can be entered into an on-line database in libraries using a computerized card catalog.

The Library of Congress Classification is a possible alternative but seems cumbersome for use in any but the largest collections. It may be appropriate in college and university libraries where the books and other media are cataloged according to this system and the intention is to maintain uniformity in handling all types of media. Again, complete sets of catalog cards can be prepared, or the information can be entered into an on-line database.

Today's technology makes it possible to develop a non-line catalog rather than the traditional card catalog or a book catalog. Several computerized catalog programs are now being marketed for use in school library media centers. A good database management program can be adapted for searching a small collection. Computer access can be by program title, diskette/tape/cartridge title, subject, grade level, microcomputer system(s), type of program, publisher, etc. Electronic catalogs offer the possibility of access from a variety of sites, the capability of printing subject bibliographies on demand, and the option of searching by many more fields than is possible with the traditional card catalog.

Printed catalog cards for microcomputer courseware are not yet generally available, although a few publishers and distributors now offer catalog card sets with courseware packages. The sample cards in this chapter are included as guidelines that can be adapted to meet local needs. The format is based on the *Anglo-American Cataloguing Rules,* 2nd edition, published by the American Library Association. However, the description "machine-readable data file" has been changed to "microcomputer program" as possibly a more appropriate term for the school library media center.

Catalog cards for courseware will be similar to those for books and other media in many respects. The main entry (top line of the master card) will usually be the title of the diskette, tape, or cartridge. Additional title entries may be needed when there is more than one program on a diskette/tape/cartridge. An author card is desirable when the author, or person primarily responsible for the intellectual content of the program, can be identified.

```
MCP      Moptown (Microcomputer program) / Leslie M.
793.7    Grimm ; graphics by Corinne Grimm ; manual
MO       by Teri H. Perl. -- Cupertino, CA : Apple
         Computer, c1981.
         11 programs (on 1 5¼ in. diskette), 1 guide

         System requirements:  Apple II or II+, 48K,
         3.3 DOS, Applesoft BASIC, 1 disk drive, color
         monitor

         A series of logic games in graduated
         levels of difficulty.

1 Logic    2 Educational games    3 English language
I Grimm, Leslie    II Grimm, Corinne    III Title
```

Sample title card for the Library Media Center.

```
         Grimm, Leslie M.
MCP      Moptown (Microcomputer program) / Leslie M.
793.7    Grimm ; graphics by Corinne Grimm ; manual
MO       by Teri H. Perl. -- Cupertino, CA : Apple
         Computer, c1981.
         11 programs (on 1 5¼ in. diskette), 1 guide

         System requirements:  Apple II or II+, 48K,
         3.3 DOS, Applesoft BASIC, 1 disk drive, color
         monitor

         A series of logic games in graduated
         levels of difficulty.

1 Logic    2 Educational games    3 English language
I Grimm, Leslie                   II Grimm, Corinne
III Title
```

Sample author card for the Library Media Center.

Determining the copyright date of the program is often difficult. When several programs in a package have different copyright dates it is preferable to use the copyright date on the diskette/tape/cartridge or on the documentation.

Some library media centers place a color band across the top of the catalog card to indicate audio-visual materials. Microcomputer courseware would seem to fit logically into the audio-visual category, making the use of a color band appropriate in these collections.

Many library media specialists choose to indicate the type of media by some notation above the call number. The simplest method, from the user's point of view, is to use the words MICROCOMPUTER PROGRAM (or COMPUTER PROGRAM). A small stamp fits better than typing the words. An alternative is to type the letters MCP (or CP) above the call number. Another alternative is the use of COMPUTER PROGRAM as a subheading on each subject card, e.g., OREGON TRAIL—COMPUTER PROGRAM. In many card catalogs, however, no special notation is used to identify the format.

The subjects used to describe the contents of the courseware in the catalog can be taken from either of two standard library guides: *Sears List of Subject Headings or Library of Congress Subject Headings*. If desired, an added subject can be used to indicate the type of program. Examples would be COMPUTER SIMULATIONS or COMPUTER DRILL & PRACTICE; these can also be used as subheadings. As with any cataloging, it is important that written records be kept to provide consistency in the use of subject headings. This is especially important if the list of subjects is developed locally. All cataloging information should be added to your processing manual.

The physical description of the courseware also needs to be standardized. Decisions should be made regarding which terms to use:

a. Floppy disk, hard disk, disk, or diskette
b. Cassette tape, computer tape, or tape
c. Cartridge
d. Documentation, manual, guide, or instructions

```
            WORD GAMES
  MCP     Crossword magic (Microcomputer program). --
  793.7     Version 2.0 -- Sunnyvale, CA. : L & S
  CR        Computerware, c1982.
            7 programs (on 2 5¼ in. diskettes), 1 guide

            System requirements:  Apple II or II+,
            48K, 3.3 DOS, Applesoft BASIC, 1 disk drive,
            printer

            User can create, edit, print, and save
            up to 20 puzzles from user chosen words.

  1 Crossword puzzles      2 Word games
```

Sample subject card for the Library Media Center.

Other items to include in the description are brand and model of microcomputer, amount of memory required, peripherals needed, computer language, DOS version, and an itemized documentation list. It is also useful to indicate whether the program is available for other microcomputers or in a different format (tape or diskette, for example) and to give a brief descriptive summary of the program.

Catalog cards can be filed with other cards in the library media center card catalog. Duplicate cards can be prepared as needed for use in the computer lab or in other areas.

COURSEWARE IN THE PROFESSIONAL LIBRARY OR DISPLAY CENTER

A large courseware collection in a professional library designed for use by teachers and other educators can be arranged according to the pattern outlined above for library media centers. This works especially well when the collection is part of a professional library and users are accustomed to browsing for materials they need.

In display centers the programs can be divided by subject to help the users locate materials quickly without needing to refer to a card catalog or other library index. One easy method is to use colored folders, colored labels, or some other color coding to designate each subject: red for science, blue for language arts, green for math, etc. Users can immediately identify the subject of each package by the color.

Subjects can also be designated by the use of key words: Art, Science, Math, etc. The subject word can be stamped on the front cover and on the spine of each package. Collections that already use color coding to separate programs according to different computer systems will find key word subject identification especially useful.

The programs within each subject can be arranged alphabetically by title or in some type of numerical order. An identification number can be used to subdivide each subject into smaller topics. Packages keyed red for science, for example, can be numbered sequentially to denote biology (3.0-3.9), physics (4.0-4.9), chemistry (5.0-5.9), etc. A subject classification system used to organize a film library can also be adapted for use in a courseware collection.

Again we have the problem of how to handle the diskette, tape, or cartridge that contains more than one program. Math, language arts, and science programs are often combined in one package, creating difficulties when shelving, cataloging and/or color-coding by subject. Often the most useful subject in the package will be selected for shelving purposes, with other subjects also listed in the index file or catalog.

There is always a fine line between convenience in devising a really useful yet simple subject or color-coding system and the development of a system that is too complex for anyone to understand or use easily. Any subject arrangement, whether using colors, words, or other devices, also runs the risk of being either too general or too detailed to be satisfactory to the users.

Sets of catalog cards can be filed in the main card catalog of a professional library, or data can be entered into an on-line catalog. For a display center, either an on-line catalog using a database management program or one of the software library, or data can be entered into an on-line catalog. For a display center, either an on-line catalog using a database management program or one of the software library catalog programs frequently printed in computer journals can be used to Simplicity of use and ease of maintenance should be the criteria used in deciding which of these options to use.

Chapter 14

Processing the Courseware

The efficient management of the courseware collection requires careful attention to processing. Important factors to consider are ease of maintenance and protection of the diskettes and tapes. The cost of processing materials and the amount of labor involved also help determine which methods to use.

PACKAGING

Courseware can most easily be left in the original packaging. This works well if the courseware is being stored in file drawers, in numerical or alphabetical order by title, with each package in a separate file folder or envelope. These become a form of packaging and can be numbered, color coded, etc., according to the system of arrangement being used.

A similar approach is to put the smaller packages into light cardboard folders with side pockets. The diskette or tape can go into the pocket on one side and the documentation into the other pocket. The folders can be shelved individually, or several folders can be put into a pamphlet file box as described below. Folders can also be stored upright in bins similar to those used for record displays.

Some collections will include courseware for more than one brand of computer and/or for different models. It is helpful to use a different color for each brand or model, especially if the packages are shelved together. Colored cardboard folders can be adapted to a color-coding scheme to indicate either subject or microcomputer brand.

Diskette and documentation packaged in a lightweight cardboard folder.

Special large cardboard media boxes (available from library supply companies) can be used effectively to store the courseware, especially in cases where it is important to have uniform packaging. The larger boxes can accommodate the large three-ring binders used to package some software and documentation. The media boxes are easy to shelve, stand up well to heavy circulation, and provide good protection to prevent bending of the diskettes. They are also the most expensive form of packaging suggested here and require the most shelf space.

A practical arrangement that works especially well for larger collections is the combination of several sizes of binders, cardboard folders, and media boxes on the shelves. Courseware packages that arrive in sturdy binders can then be shelved as is with only the addition of labels, color-coding, and other necessary markings. An occasional media box can be used when the documentation is unwieldy or too large for a binder. Cassette tapes and cartridges can be shelved in special plastic sleeves, with their documentation, in narrow three-ring binders. This combination provides some standardization as well as good protection. It is both less expensive and less wasteful of shelf space than is the purchase of special large binders or media boxes for all packages.

One question that arises is whether to store more than one courseware package in each binder. In smaller collections it may be useful to put all math packages, for example, in one large binder. If the users can check out programs to use in other areas, however, it may be better to process each package separately. Again, local needs and preferences should be considered in making the final decision.

Pamphlet file boxes can be used effectively to hold binders and folders upright on the shelves. Each file box can be clearly labeled to describe the contents, whereas labels on the folders themselves are often difficult to read. Folders are much easier to handle when shelved in the pamphlet file boxes than if they are simply standing on the shelf. File boxes can also be numbered or color-keyed to indicate the contents.

A major consideration in packaging is that the diskettes must be stored upright and must not be bent by an adjacent package, by the rings in the binder, or by poorly placed documentation within the package. One solution is to tape the diskette pocket to a piece of heavy cardboard or posterboard, leaving it open at the top to remove the diskette from the pocket. Use brightly colored cardboard, cut slightly larger than the diskette pocket, to make a sturdy backing that will also make it easier to avoid losing the pocket. This helps prevent having the diskette exposed to damage because the pocket has been lost.

Consideration must also be given to packaging or storage that will provide protection from dust. This will vary in importance depending upon whether the collection is located in a relatively dust-free room or in a more open area where there is a great deal of dust. In the latter case completely closed boxes or envelopes

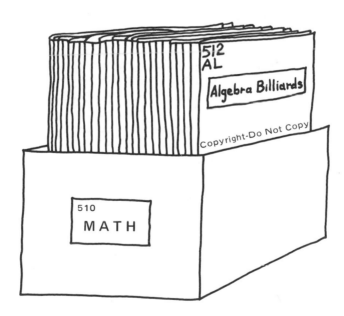

Cardboard folders for math programs are shelved in a metal pamphlet file box.

may be required to prevent damage. Diskettes and tapes need to be stored away from extreme heat or cold, and in an area protected from strong electrical or magnetic fields.

A decision must be made on whether to store the documentation separately or with the diskette, cassette, or cartridge. There are good reasons to store the teacher's manuals separately, particularly if the courseware packages are being used by individual students. A teacher may want to check out only the manual to determine whether the material meets specific classroom needs or to prepare lessons. A student may need just one diskette and one worksheet rather than the entire package. In such cases it may be necessary to devise packaging that allows only selected items to be checked out. The binder, box, etc., will usually remain in the collection to hold the items not taken. Protective packaging should be provided to hold the item(s) being checked out, and a circulation card or other record must be kept.

Documentation for programs loaded onto a hard disk system or network will need to be stored separately. In these cases there must be easy reference from the disk to any documentation for teacher or student use. Sites with networks or hard disk storage will have to plan carefully to make sure that all support materials are readily accessible to users. Packaging will need to be provided for instructions or other items in the documentation that occasionally may be needed at the computer. Copyright considerations, too, are different in these situations, and careful attention should be paid to the laws governing copying of programs.

LABELING

A uniform set of labels in a variety of sizes and shapes should be printed in a quantity that allows every item to be identified as belonging to a specific package. Large, easily read labels can be used on the front outside of each package to list the contents and the subject, classification number, identification number, or other subject code. Labels for each item of documentation can be smaller, perhaps with only the classification number or other code. Labels for diskettes, tapes, and cartridges must fit the space available.

When an identification number or accession number is assigned to a courseware package, there are two choices in labeling the contents. The same number can be used for each item, or each item can have an individualized number. For example, a package number may be 83-001, with 83 indicating the year of purchase and 001 indicating that this is the first package purchased that year. Diskette #1 is numbered 83-001A, diskette #2 is 83-001B, the teacher's guide is 83-001C, and the student's manual is 83-001D. This has the advantage of identifying each item separately while still indicating the package with which it belongs. Separate items checked out from one package can usually be listed by number more easily than by title. The numbers should be keyed to the main label that lists the entire contents by title and number. This provides a quick identification for any missing items and helps to check that returned items get into the correct package.

Placement of the outside labels will be determined by the shelving arrangement. It may be helpful to place labels on the front, in one of the upper corners, and also on the spine of wider binders. The labels should be clearly visible to make it simple for the user to locate courseware packages and to return them to their correct locations after use.

Warning labels are recommended to advise the user of the proper care of diskettes, tapes, and cartridges. Labels should also carry a copyright protection notice that warns against illegal copying.

It is often difficult to property stamp tapes, diskettes, or cartridges. Property labels can be used instead of a stamp, or the property notice can be included as part of the warning label.

Covering the labels with clear tape will attach them more securely, help to make them last longer, and prevent smudging. The extra care taken in labeling each item in the courseware package will prevent many mix-ups, losses, and other problems as the courseware is used by many students and teachers.

CIRCULATION

Some courseware will be limited to use only in the classroom, computer lab, library media center, or other area. Other programs may be checked out by students or teachers for use at home or at other sites. Professional libraries may circulate courseware to schools throughout a particular service area.

The policies governing courseware circulation must balance user needs against protection of the collection. Policies should be in writing and clearly understood by all users (see Chapter 15).

Libraries with on-line circulation systems can handle courseware as another form of media. If borrowers' cards are used, they can be attached to the courseware package or kept in a separate file at the circulation desk. A simple alternative for a classroom or lab is to maintain a written list of users, checking off borrowers as programs are returned. The essential point is to always be able to determine where a specific program is and who is using it.

Packaging must be planned to support the circulation policies. When users can check out the programs for use at home or at other sites there must be some provision for safely transporting the tape or diskette and accompanying documentation. Courseware in a sturdy box or binder can be checked out as a unit. Heavy cardboard folders work well to protect courseware shelved in lighter packages, or to hold partial contents when the entire package is not taken. Documentation checked out separately can be placed in a manila envelope or cardboard folder. The container should be clearly labeled with the contents so it can be easily checked when it is returned. A supply of circulation folders should be kept at the courseware library site. If only some items in a package are taken, a note should be inserted in the package that is left to indicate the location of the items being used. Finally, the date the materials are taken, and a return date if desired, should be indicated on the package.

The circulation system should be kept as simple as possible. The primary function is to maintain a record of where materials can be located at all times and to be able to check for any missing or damaged items when courseware is returned.

Chapter 15

A Policies and Procedures Manual

The quality and availability of the courseware collection will have a definite impact on the effectiveness with which students and teachers use microcomputers in the instructional program. Successful organization of the collection calls for creativity, ingenuity, and a willingness to be flexible. We need to make the materials readily available to the users and also to protect and preserve them for future use. A carefully developed policies and procedures manual is helpful in achieving a reasonable balance between these two goals.

The person responsible for maintaining the collection may well make the final policy decisions, but input is needed from students, teachers, administrators, and parents. Their opinions can be gathered within the formal structure of a committee or by meeting individually with interested persons. Many potential problems can be avoided by careful planning, listening to the specific needs of the users, and field-testing the procedures for access, storage, circulation, and delivery of courseware before writing the manual.

There will undoubtedly be some conflicts regarding the availability of courseware to users. It is helpful to anticipate questions that may arise and to have carefully justified answers. Policies that might otherwise be viewed as needlessly restrictive may be cooperatively accepted once they have been explained, especially if the users feel they have had some part in making the decisions. Whenever possible the policies should be approved by both administration and faculty. They should also be approved, or at least discussed, by student government representatives. Publicity in district newsletters and student publications, as well as flyers to parents, can build support for the policies governing courseware use and protection. It is especially important to gain teacher, student, and parent cooperation in respecting copyright regulations. Finally, the policies that have been adopted and publicized need to be enforced fairly and consistently.

The following outline for "A Policies and Procedures Manual" is developed as a series of numbered paragraphs grouped under appropriate headings. Some readers may be able to use specific paragraphs as written. Others may combine and adapt ideas from several paragraphs or sections to create guidelines that will meet their needs. The important concept is that each site should have a set of operating policies and procedures for the courseware collection.

**A Policies and Procedures Manual for the Microcomputer
Courseware Collection**

A. POLICY STATEMENT

1. The following policy statement shall be adopted by the school board as part of the district policy on instructional materials selection:

   Microcomputer courseware (software and the accompanying documentation) shall be selected in accordance with the established Instructional Materials Selection Policies of this district. Any citizen complaints or objections related to such materials shall be handled according to district policy regarding challenged materials.

2. Policies and procedures for the selection, organization and circulation of the microcomputer courseware collection shall be developed by a committee that includes the persons identified below.

   Teachers:
   Administrators:
   Library media specialists:
   Other staff:
   Parents:
   Students:
   Other:

3. Procedures to discourage the illegal duplication of copyrighted computer programs shall be instituted, and no illegal copies shall be made or used on school equipment.

4. Policies and procedures for the microcomputer courseware collection shall be approved by the school board and published in a manual or other set of guidelines. This information shall be publicized in district newsletters, student publications, etc., and shall be posted near the courseware collection and in other appropriate areas.

DISCUSSION: The portion of the amendment to the 1976 Copyright Reform Act relevant to the copying of computer programs is discussed in Appendix A.

The instructional materials selection policy of the American Association of School Librarians is reproduced in Appendix E.

B. SELECTION

1. Selection of courseware shall be the responsibility of a committee that includes:

2. Purchase orders for courseware to be previewed shall be requested by the selection committee identified in Part B-1 and shall be processed by the business office. Courseware purchases' shall be funded from account(s) #----.

C. EVALUATION

1. Courseware shall be evaluated using the following form(s):

   (Select forms from Appendix B.)

2. Courseware shall be evaluated by a committee established by the selection committee identified in Part B-1.

3. The evaluation process shall include the following steps:

   (See Chapter 12.)

4. Results of the evaluation process shall be used as the basis for a purchase decision.

D. ORDERING

1. Courseware shall be ordered as stated in Part B-2.

2. Courseware shall be ordered from selected jobber(s) and/or publisher(s) according to specific needs.

3. All courseware shall be sent immediately to the person responsible for processing. No courseware shall be sent directly to the classroom, computer lab, or other site until it has been processed. When a decision is made to keep courseware that has been received for preview, it shall be processed before it is made available for general use.

4. Purchase orders and invoices shall be checked and processed in accordance with established business office policies.

5. Courseware shall be inventoried, cataloged, packaged and labeled as part of the processing procedure outlined in Part E.

E. PROCESSING

1. All courseware packages shall be processed before they are used in the schools. Packages shall be sent to _____ for processing.

2. One back-up (archival) copy of each diskette and tape shall be made if possible, or ordered separately, if it is not provided with the original order. Back-up copies shall be processed with the entire package but shall be clearly labeled "Back-up copy—For archival use only" and shall be packaged separately.

3. Cataloging information shall be assigned as needed.

4. Courseware shall be labeled and packaged. Catalog cards shall be prepared as needed.

5. Inventory records shall be updated at the school or other site.

6. Processed courseware shall be sent to the school, computer lab, classroom, library media center, or other area where it is to be kept. The back-up copy shall be stored in the archival collection; it is not to be available for general use.

7. Lists of newly received courseware shall be distributed to all interested personnel.

F. SEARCHING THE COLLECTION

1. Users will be able to locate courseware by searching:

   An on-line database
   A card catalog
   A catalog in book format
   A subject index
   A list of titles
   Other

2. Courseware will be listed or indexed by:

   Program title
   Package title
   Subject area(s)
   Type of program
   Grade level(s)
   Computer system(s)
   Publisher
   Other

G. ACCESSIBILITY

1. Access to the courseware collection will be available to the following users:

   Teachers
   Administrators
   Library media specialists
   Staff
   Aides
   Students
   Parents
   Community members
   Other

2. Courseware can be used at the following specified locations:

   Classroom
   Computer lab
   Library media center
   Anywhere in the school
   District office
   District instructional media center or computing center
   All schools in the district
   Anywhere in the district or region
   Checked out by teacher for home use
   Checked out by student for home use

3. Users shall be asked to demonstrate a specified minimum level of competence before using courseware.

4. Courseware may be kept by the user:

   For the class period
   For the school day
   For overnight use
   For 3 days
   For 1 week
   Until another user requests it
   Indefinitely
   Other

5. Damage to the courseware shall be paid for as determined by local policy.

6. Courseware will be checked out to users by:

   Signing an individual checkout card kept with each package
   Completing a Courseware Checkout Form
   Signing a list of current users
   Entering the user's name into an electronic record of courseware users

7. Users may be asked to return a specific courseware package if another user is waiting for it.

8. Teachers (have, do not have) priority over students when both want the same courseware.

9. Documentation intended for the teacher shall not be checked out to students.

10. Each courseware package shall be checked for complete contents and for damage when it is returned.

DISCUSSION: The user policies should be as liberal as possible to encourage the use of the collection while still maintaining the control necessary to minimize damage and loss.

A totally different situation exists when the expanded storage capacity of a hard disk is available. The actual programs may all be on the disk, with only the documentation being stored locally for circulation to students and/or teachers. Networking systems also require special planning for the way in which the software and documentation will be accessed and stored.

H. STORAGE

1. The courseware collection will be located in:

   Classroom(s)
   Library media center
   Computer lab
   Office
   District office
   County or regional office
   Other

2. Courseware packages will be stored upright:

   On shelves
   In file drawers, cabinets, or bins
   or
   Courseware will be loaded onto a hard disk with the documentation stored separately

3. Courseware packages will be arranged according to the system selected:

   Subject coding by word or color
   Color coding
   Dewey Decimal Classification
   Library of Congress Classification
   Computer brand or model
   Other

4. Courseware will be kept in a dust-free area that is protected from excessive heat, magnetic fields, strong electrical currents, or other factors that may cause damage.

Courseware Directory

COURSEWARE DIRECTORY

Courseware entries are arranged in alphabetical order by title, followed by the microcomputer(s) on which the program runs, subject area, and a descriptive annotation. Documentation usually refers to printed materials that accompany the program. Cataloging information provides a Dewey Decmial number and a subject heading; sources are *Sears List of Subject Headings,* 11th edition (H.W. Wilson Company, 1977) and the *Abridged Dewey Decimal Classification and Relative Index,* 10th edition (Forest Press, Inc., 1971). The publisher is next, followed by the diskette title in parentheses whenever that title differs from the program title cited in the text.

The recommendations from other journals are listed in alphabetical order by journal title. A citation is included ONLY if it is a critical review with a favorable recommendation. No negative reviews are included. Therefore, the appearance of a journal title in the RECOMMENDED list indicates that the program received a positive review in that issue of the journal.

SAMPLE ENTRY:

Program title (or Diskette title) as cited in text
Microcomputer(s)
Subject area
Descriptive annotation
Documentation
Cataloging information
Publisher (followed by Diskette title if that is different from the program title cited in the text)
Recommended favorably by the journal(s) listed   **115**

COURSEWARE SELECTIONS

ADDITION—ALL LEVELS / SUBTRACTION—ALL LEVELS

PET   Math

Addition (24 skill levels) and subtraction (12 skill levels) drill for grades 1-6. Problems are presented vertically and student enters answers from right to left. Graphic rewards for correct responses enhance the program.

Documentation: Teacher's guide with instructions for changing time limits and levels of difficulty.

Cataloging: 513   Arithmetic

Publisher: Teaching Tools: Microcomputer Services

Recommended: Creative Computing   October 1981
Creative Computing   February 1982
Kilobaud Microcomputing   June 1981
Midnight Software Gazette   Summer 1981
School Microware Reviews   Winter 1982
School Microware Reviews   Summer 1982

ALGEBRA BILLIARDS

TRS-80   Math

Students solve algebraic equations within the motivational framework of a scored billiard game. Program automatically adjusts difficulty level in response to student performance and teacher can control number ranges.

Documentation: Teacher's guide and program description.

Cataloging: 512   Algebra

Publisher: Curriculum Applications

Recommended: The Computing Teacher   Vol. 8 No. 6
Mathematics Teacher   April 1982
Purser's Magazine   Winter 1981
School Microware Reviews   Summer 1981
School Microware Reviews   Winter 1982

ALPHABET

PET   Language Arts

Displays seven consecutive letters of the alphabet with one blank and student must supply missing letter. Good prompts in response to errors.

Documentation: Instructions and sample run.

Cataloging: 411   Alphabet

Publisher: Microcomputers in Education

Recommended: Journal of Learning Disabilities   October 1982

ALPHABETIZE

Apple, PET, TRS-80   Language Arts

Three to eight words are presented on the screen in a numbered list and the student exchanges words by their numbers until they are in correct alphabetical order. A clock in the upper corner of the screen times the students and challenges them to improve their scores by competing with themselves.

Documentation: Teacher's guide with instructions for entering individualized word lists, sample program run and listing, suggested classroom uses, and student activitiy sheets.

Cataloging: 411   Alphabet

Publisher: School CourseWare Journal (Nov/Dec 1981)

ALPHAKEY

TRS-80   Primary

Keyboard alphabet practice for preschool and primary grades. Teacher summary reports score and identifies errors for each user.

Documentation: Instruction manual.

Cataloging: 411   Alphabet

Publisher: Radio Shack

Recommended: Chicatrug News   December 1980

AMAZING

Apple   Language Arts

Designs and prints word mazes using teacher or student generated word lists. Maze size can vary from 3 x 3 to 25 x 32. Printer is required.

Documentation: Teacher's guide and suggested classroom activities.

Cataloging: 793.7   Word games

Publisher: MECC (Elementary Vol. 2)

Recommended: JEM Reference Manual   Vol. I Release II
                        MACUL Journal   Winter 1981

AMAZING

TRS-80 Color Computer   Logic

Program displays a maze briefly and student then enters the maze, seeing the walls from a rat's viewpoint. Goal is to escape from the maze without needing to return to the original display for help.

Documentation: Instructions in program.

Cataloging: 793.7   Puzzles

Publisher: Chromasette (March 1982)

APPLE LOGO

Apple   Computer Science

This is the complete LOGO language as developed by Logo Computer Systems, Inc. At the introductory level the language functions in the graphics mode with the "screen turtle". Children are encouraged to explore the entire learning process. Beyond Turtle Graphics, LOGO is a complete, complex, and innovative computer language.

Documentation: Reference Manual; Introduction to Programming Through Turtle Graphics.

Cataloging: 400.28   Programming languages (Electronic computers)

Publisher: Apple Computer, Inc.

Recommended: Booklist   September 1, 1982

APPLE PILOT

Apple   Teacher Utility

This Apple version of Common PILOT is a complex, powerful and flexible computer language designed to help teachers develop their own courseware. Includes graphics editor, character set editor, and sound editor to enhance the lessons developed.

Documentation: Reference Manual and user's manual.

Cataloging: 400.28   Programming languages (Electronic computers)

Publisher: Apple Computer, Inc.

Recommended: Creative Computing   July 1982
              Educational Technology   March 1982
              Micro-Scope   September 1981
              Purser's Magazine   Winter 1981
              Softalk   May 1981

APPLE PRESENTS APPLE

Apple   Computer Science

Tutorial introduction to the Apple keyboard leads students through a carefully structured series of exercises.

Documentation: In program.

Cataloging: 652.3   Typewriting

Publisher: Apple Computer, Inc.

ATARI PILOT

Atari   Computer Science

Atari PILOT combines Turtle Graphics from LOGO with PILOT text handling and the sound and color capability of the Atari to create an introductory computer language for children.

Documentation: Student manual and teacher's guide.

Cataloging: 400.28   Programming languages (Electronic computers)

Publisher: Atari

Recommended: Atari Computer Enthusiasts   June 1982
              CUE Newsletter   May 15, 1982
              Electronic Education   November 1981
              Curriculum Review   October 1982
              School Microware Reviews   Summer 1982

BASIC ELECTRICITY

Apple   Science

Graphic demonstration of flow of electricity, open and closed circuits, short circuits. Student can choose demonstration, lesson, puzzle to solve, or test.

Documentation: Instructions.

Cataloging: 537   Electricity

Publisher: Ideatech

Apple   Teacher Utility

Complex authoring system designed to help teachers create lessons in any subject area, with provisions for both text and testing. Several hundred graphics included in the system can be inserted into lessons. Teachers can also use the graphics package to create new illustrations.

Documentation: User's manual with complete instructions, illustrations, and sample lessons.

Cataloging: 400.28   Authoring systems

Publisher: California School for the Deaf

Recommended: Compute!   April 1982

Bumble Games

Apple, Atari   Math

Six programs introducing young children to the use of number pairs to name positions in arrays and grids. Color graphics, sound, and music contribute to the fun of these learning games.

Documentation: Manual designed for the child to use as a guide to the games; activity cards.

Cataloging: 513   Arithmetic

Publisher: The Learning Company

Recommended: Compute!   May 1982

USER'S   November 1982

Bumble Plot

Apple, Atari   Math

Developmental series of learning games that uses positive and negative numbers in advancing the graphing skills introduced in Bumble Games.

Documentation: Manual designed for the child to use as a guide to the games; activity cards.

Cataloging: 513   Arithmetic

Publisher: The Learning Company

Recommended: USER'S   November 1982

TRS-80   Teacher Utility

Complex authoring system that can be used to create lesson materials in any subject area. It includes tutorial and testing modes, graphics, and a student record-keeping function. Student responses can be formatted for multiple-choice, true-false or completion questions.

Documentation: Manual with instructions for teachers to aid in developing materials and instructions for student use of the lessons.

Cataloging: 400.28   Authoring systems

Publisher: MicroGnome

Recommended: Educational Technology   April 1982
             80 Microcomputing   February 1982
             Interface Age   May 1982
             Purser's Magazine   Fall 1981

CALENDAR SKILLS

Apple   Math

Students type in answers to questions about months, days, seasons, holidays, and abbreviations in ten lessons of twenty questions each. Teachers can enter new questions as needed. Records errors for teacher's file.

Documentation: Teacher's manual and instructions.

Cataloging: 529   Calendars

Publisher: Hartley Courseware, Inc.

Recommended: Apple Journal of Courseware Review   Issue 1

CATERPILLAR

Apple, Atari   Language Arts

Colorful drill on alphabetical sequence of letters, with segments of the caterpillar being added for each correct answer. Other programs on the disk include Train, Sounds, Pictures, Words, Shapes, Smile, Wuzzle, and Spaceships.

Documentation: Teacher's guide, student materials, instructions.

Cataloging: 411   Alphabet

Publisher: MECC (Apple: Elementary Vol. 7; Atari: Primary Pre-Reading)

Apple, Atari   Science

Three titration simulations for advanced secondary or college students: Acid-base titration, Avogadro's number, Weak acid equilibrium constant. Student controls the titration process and must calculate correct values or repeat the experiment.

Documentation: Detailed instructions are built into the program and repeated in the manual. Manual provides theoretical background for the experiments, sample demonstrations and notes.

Cataloging: 540.7   Chemistry-Experiments

Publisher: High Technology, Inc.

Recommended: Creative Computing   September 1980
                InfoWorld   October 13, 1980
                JEM Reference Manual   Vol. I Release II

CLASSROOM MONITOR

Apple   Teacher Utility

Utility program for a disk-sharing system that allows all students to view a teacher demonstration simultaneously on their own screens, allows the teacher to monitor individual student work from a central station, and provides access to a printer from all student stations.

Documentation: Manual and tutorial.

Cataloging: 001.6   Computer programs

Publisher: Software Connections

CLOCK

Apple   Math

Telling time by setting the hands on the screen clock to correspond to time presented on the screen either digitally or in words, and also by typing in the digital time in response to a clock face.

Documentation: Teacher's guide, instructions for keeping student records.

Cataloging: 681   Clocks and watches

Publisher: Hartley Courseware, Inc.

Recommended: Apple Journal of Courseware Review   Issue 1
                Arithmetic Teacher   April 1982
                Booklist   October 1, 1981
                JEM Reference Manual   Vol. I Release II

Purser's Magazine   Spring 1980
School Microware Reviews   Winter 1982

COMPUPOEM

Apple   Language Arts

Encourages students to create original poems using various structures provided by the computer as prompts.

Documentation: Instructions and sample poems.

Cataloging: 808.1   Poetics

Publisher: Compupoem

COMPUTER DISCOVERY

Apple, Atari, TRS-80   Computer Science

Highly creative introduction to computer awareness and to simple programming. Accompanying computer programs are NOT strictly math oriented but are designed to meet a wide range of student interests. Separate versions are available for junior and senior high school.

Documentation: Teacher's guide, suggested resources, and workbooks for both levels.

Cataloging: 621.3819   Computer awareness

Publisher: Science Research Associates

Recommended: AEDS Monitor   November 1981
            Curriculum Review   August/September 1982
            Educational Computer   September/October 1982
            Electronic Learning   September/October 1981
            Journal of Courseware Review   Vol. 1 No. 1
            USER'S   May 1981

COMPUTER DRILL & INSTRUCTION: MATHEMATICS

Apple, Atari   Math

Management system that controls student progress through a structured sequence of lessons in basic arithmetic skills: number concepts, addition, subtraction, multiplication, division, fractions, and decimals. Diagnostic placement tests determine student's entry point, and student is shifted to easier or more difficult material in response to performance. Student scores are recorded for teacher use.

Documentation: Teacher's manual with objectives and instructions for using the system in the classroom.

Cataloging: 513   Arithmetic

Publisher: Science Research Associates

Recommended: Educational Computer   September/October 1982
EPIE Report   98/99m

CO-PILOT

Apple   Teacher Utility

Tutorial designed to teach the novice user how to use Apple PILOT to develop instructional activities on the computer, including the utilization of sound and graphics. Users do not need to know how to program.

Documentation: User's manual.

Cataloging: 400.28   Authoring systems

Publisher: Apple Computer, Inc.

CROSSBOW

PET   Math

Student shoots arrow at a point on a line segment between 0 and 1 and attempts to identify the correct fraction represented by that point. Line is divided into fractions of increasing difficulty.

Documentation: Instructions.

Cataloging: 513   Arithmetic

Publisher: Hayden Book Company, Inc.

Recommended: The Computing Teacher   Vol. 7 No. 6

CROSS CLUES

Apple   Language Arts

Logical thinking, spelling skill, and luck are all needed in this word game for two players. Players may choose from 50 different games and the novice is offered an initial demonstration that clearly explains rules and strategy. Consonant clues are given to help players complete words on a crossword puzzle type grid. Scoring and timing are monitored by the computer and displayed on the screen.

Documentation: Game instructions.

Cataloging: 793.7   Word games

Publisher: Science Research Associates

Recommended: Creative Computing   April 1982
Educational Computer   March/April 1982
InfoWorld   December 14, 1981

CROSSWORD MAGIC

Apple, Atari   Language Arts

User constructs crossword puzzles ranging in size up to 20 x 20 spaces, entering one word at a time which the program places into the puzzle grid. User then writes clues up to 98 characters long. The completed puzzle can be printed on paper or displayed on the computer screen. Numbers can be used instead of letters to create a math puzzle.

Documentation: Instruction pamphlet.

Cataloging: 793.73   Crossword puzzles

Publisher: L & S Computerware

Recommended: Booklist   September 1, 1982
Classroom Computer News   March/April 1982
Courseware Report Card   September 1982
Creative Computing   April 1982
InfoWorld   October 18, 1982
Educational Computer   November/December 1982
Peelings II   January 1982

DARTS

Apple   Math

Game format provides effective practice with equivalent fractions and develops skill in estimating fractions at several difficulty levels. Use of randomly generated line lengths makes each game different. Two levels of difficulty are available.

Documentation: Teacher's guide.

Cataloging: 513   Arithmetic

Publisher: Apple Computer, Inc. (Elementary, My Dear Apple)

Recommended: Classroom Computer News   March/April 1982
                Popular Computing   November 1981
                Purser's Magazine   Winter 1981

DIET

Apple, Atari, PET, TRS-80   Science

Simulates adjustments in diet to improve nutrition or to change weight. Students can record the food eaten each day and enter their physical characteristics to determine potentially beneficial diet changes. Other simulations on disk include Pollute, Rats, and Malaria.

Documentation: Instructions.

Cataloging: 641.1   Nutrition

Publisher: Creative Computing

Recommended: The Computing Teacher   December 1981
                Creative Computing   September 1980
                Mathematics Teacher   October 1981
                Peelings II   January 1982

DIVISION SKILLS

Apple   Math

Student begins with basic skills at an introductory level and progresses through a series of topics designed for grades 6-8. Teacher or student may select any number of problems from 10 to 90 and set the speed of presentation.

Documentation: Teacher's manual with instructions for using the management system to pre-test and assign students to appropriate levels, task cards, and duplicating masters.

Cataloging: 513   Arithmetic

Publisher: Milton Bradley
Recommended: Courseware Report Card   September 1982
                Mathematics Teacher   November 1981
                Media & Methods   March 1982

ECOLOGY SIMULATIONS 1 & 2

Apple, Atari, PET, TRS-80   Science

Simulations that involve students in various long-term studies related to the environment. Disk 1: Sterl explores the use of pesticides and the release of sterile males for pest control; Pop demonstrates three models of population projection; Tag (see below); Buffalo simulates growth and decline of a herd. Disk 2: Pollute investigates water pollution; Rats explores sanitation and fast or slow poison for rat control; Malaria simulates attempts to control an epidemic; Diet (see above).

Documentation: Instructions.

Cataloging: 574.5   Ecology

Publisher: Creative Computing

Recommended: The Computing Teacher   December 1981
Creative Computing   September 1980, May 1981
Mathematics Teacher   October 1981, April 1982
MACUL Journal   Spring 1980
Peelings II   January 1982
Purser's Magazine   Fall 1979

ENGINE

Apple   Science

Animated operation of a four-cycle engine shows intake, compression, power, and exhaust cycles. Motion can be manually controlled for demonstrations.

Documentation: Instructions.

Cataloging: 621.4   Engines

Publisher: Apple Computer, Inc.

Recommended: MACUL Journal   Spring 1980

ESSENTIAL MATH—VOLUMES 1 & 2

TRS-80   Math

Math management package for the secondary school offers a placement mode to determine where student should enter the system and a skill building mode with automatic promotion and demotion based upon performance. Vol. 1 provides practice with number concepts, addition, subtraction, multiplication, and division. Fractions, decimals, percent, and pre-algebra concepts are covered in Vol. 2.

Documentation: Teacher's guide with objectives, operating instructions, lesson content summaries, and a description of the automatic student placement system.

Cataloging: 513   Arithmetic

Publisher: Radio Shack

FACTORING WHOLE NUMBERS

Apple, TRS-80   Math

12 programs introduce factor pairs, primes and composites, exponents, highest common factor, and least common factor. One program provides a drill review for each topic and another program gives additional practice in the form of creative and unusual games and contests. Highly interactive, with challenging material for advanced students.

Documentation: Teacher's guide with descriptions of programs, objectives, educational philosophy of the lessons, and suggested enrichment activities.

Cataloging: 510   Mathematics

Publisher: QED (Quality Educational Designs)

Recommended: The Computing Teacher   Vol. 8 No. 4
             The Computing Teacher   Vol. 9 No. 4
             CUE Newsletter   October 1, 1980
             Mathematics Teacher   October 1981
             MicroSIFT   January 1982
             USER'S   November 1981

FRACTION-EQUIV 1

PET   Math

Practice in finding the equivalent of a given fraction, either reducing it to the lowest terms or finding the equivalent for a fraction already reduced. Unusually good response to errors graphically demonstrates the correct response in successively simpler ways each time the student gives the wrong answer and will not continue the program until the student enters correct answer. Large clear numerals.

Documentation: Instructions and sample run.

Cataloging: 513   Arithmetic

Publisher: Microcomputers in Education

Recommended: Classroom Computer News   September/October 1982

FRACTIONS

Apple, TRS-80   Math

Basic concepts, operations, measurement and compound fractions are presented in highly interactive instructional sequences and in challenging games.

Documentation: Teacher's guide with program descriptions, instructional objectives, suggested teaching techniques, and related enrichment activities.

Cataloging: 513 Arithmetic

Publisher: QED (Quality Educational Designs)

Recommended: The Computing Teacher   Vol. 8 No. 4
        CUE Newsletter   October 1, 1980
        Mathematics Teacher   October 1981
        MicroSIFT   January 1982
        School Microwave Reviews   Winter 1982

FROG!

PET   Primary

Young children teach the frog how to catch bugs by pressing the number keys. Develops eye-hand coordination and logical thinking skills as the child has fun learning to use the computer.

Documentation: Instructions.

Cataloging: 793.7 Puzzles

Publisher: CURSOR (#19   April 1980)

Recommended: Compute!   May 1982

FUNCTION GRAPHER

Apple   Math

Uses coefficients supplied by students to draw graphs for polynomial, trigonometric, logarithmic, and exponential functions. Two functions can be graphed on the same set of axes.

Documentation: Description and operating instructions.

Cataloging: 510 Mathematics

Publisher: Math Software
        Journal of Computers in Mathematics and Science Teaching   Spring 1982
        Mathematics Teacher   February 1982

Recommended: MicroSIFT   October 1981

FUNDAMENTAL PUNCTUATION PRACTICE

Apple, TRS-80   Language Arts

Instruction and practice with 50 lessons on commas, periods, and other ending punctuation, apostrophes, abbreviations and initials, quotations, addresses, and other punctuation marks. Student management system records performance and prints reports.

Documentation: Teacher's manual with instructional objectives and instructions.

Cataloging: 421   Punctuation

Publisher: Random House

FUR TRADER

PET   Social Studies

Simulated fur trading expedition across Canada by canoe in 1779. Students purchase supplies, plan their route, make decisions on trading values, and handle problems that arise during the trip.

Documentation: Instructions.

Cataloging: 338.3   Fur trade

Publisher: Creative Computing   (Sensational Simulations)

FURS

Atari   Social Studies

Fur trading simulation set in Minnesota and Ontario during early 1800s. Students plan the canoe trip and attempt to arrive at the rendezvous in the least possible time and with the largest possible number of furs. Decisions must be made about supplies, travel time, trading, and dealing with hazards of the trip.

Documentation: Teacher's guide with objectives and instructions, student worksheets and suggested activities.

Cataloging: 338.3   Fur trade

Publisher: MECC   (American History)

GALAXY MATH FACTS GAME

Apple, TRS-80   Math

The student answers basic math facts in addition, subtraction, multiplication, and division to accumulate the energy and ammunition needed to pilot a space craft safely back to earth. Program automatically adjusts to student's ability level.

Documentation: Teacher's guide with objectives and instructions.

Cataloging: 513   Arithmetic

Publisher: Random House

GAME SHOW

Apple   Teacher Utility

TV game show format pits two teams against each other using screen graphics that include two players and the host. Clues are given to alternate teams and the winner who guesses the correct answer receives a cash reward. There are 18 categories in the game and teachers can add new categories and/or questions.

Documentation: Instruction manual.

Cataloging: 793.7   Puzzles

Publisher: Computer-Advanced Ideas, Inc.

Recommended: Booklist   September 1, 1982
             Educational Technology   May 1982

GEOGRAPHY EXPLORER USA

TRS-80   Social Studies

Displays regional maps of U.S. and quizzes students about state names, capitals, abbreviations, largest cities, and nicknames. Questions give state name and request information or give information and request state name. Teacher can limit which of seven regions will be presented.

Documentation: Teacher's guide with instructions for using program, directions for student, objectives and worksheets.

Cataloging: 917.3   U.S. - Geography

Publisher: Instant Software, Inc.

Recommended: Purser's Magazine   Winter 1981
             MicroSIFT   January 1982
             School Microware Reviews   Summer 1982

GEOGRAPHY SEARCH

Apple, TRS-80   Social Studies

Students are crew members embarking on a voyage of discovery in search of a new continent and a city of gold. Successful adventurers return with a ship of gold for the Queen. Students must buy provisions for the voyage, determine latitude and longitude, and cope with winds and weather.

Documentation: Search Book includes all background information necessary for students to use the program. Teacher's manual repeats the information in the student's Search Book and also has suggested classroom activities, a sample run, and pictures of selected screens.

Cataloging: 910   Discoveries (in geography)

Publisher: McGraw-Hill

Recommended: Apple Journal of Courseware Review Issue 1
             Classroom Computer News   January/February 1982
             Electronic Learning   January/February 1982
             School Microware Reviews   Summer 1981

GEOLOGY SEARCH

Apple, TRS-80   Science

Simulated oil exploration in which students select sites for drilling, handle finances of selling oil to fund additional prospecting, and learn to make decisions based on a thorough understanding of geological formations and modern technology.

Documentation: Search Book includes all background information necessary for students to use the program. Teacher's manual repeats the information in the student's Search Book and also has suggested classroom activities, a sample run, and pictures of selected screens.

Cataloging: 553   Petroleum - Geology

Publisher: McGraw-Hill

Recommended: Softalk   October 1982
             USER'S   September 1982

GEOMETRY AND MEASUREMENT DRILL AND PRACTICE

Apple   Math

Basic skills practice to supplement instructions in measurement and introductory geometry: classifying polygons, measuring line segments, telling time, perimeter, volume, and area. Uses randomly generated problems and graphic illustrations.

Documentation: Teacher's manual includes objectives, instructions, sample runs and screen displays, definitions, and student record sheets.

Cataloging: 516   Geometry

Publisher: Apple Computer, Inc.

Recommended: Journal of Courseware Review   Vol. 1 No. 1
School Microware Reviews   Winter 1982
Softalk   January 1982

Gertrude's Puzzles

Apple, Atari   Logic

Children develop problem solving and reasoning skills as they explore Gertrude's game rooms. They enjoy manipulating the colors and shapes to discover the patterns involved in each game.

Documentation: Child's guide to Gertrude's world with instructions and map; activity cards.

Cataloging: 793.7   Puzzles

Publisher: The Learning Company

Recommended: USER'S   November 1982

Haber (Chemical Equilibrium)

Apple, PET, TRS-80   Science

Highly interactive demonstration of the Haber process of producing ammonia from hydrogen and nitrogen. For advanced high school and college students.

Documentation: Teacher's guide and student supplement with operating instructions.

Cataloging: 540.7   Chemistry - Experiments

Publisher: CONDUIT

Recommended: Journal of Computers in Mathematics and Science
Teaching   Winter 1981
Journal of Courseware Review   Vol. 1 No. 1

Hammurabi

PET   Social Studies

Student becomes the ruler of ancient Sumeria in a simulation where decisions about resources management either enlarge or destroy the country's population.

Documentation: Instructions.

Cataloging: 338.9   Economic policy

Publisher: Creative Computing (Sensational Simulations)

HODGE PODGE

Apple   Primary

Young children can investigate the keyboard by pressing each separate key to activate a short colorful program illustrating a verb or noun associated with that letter or number. Many have sound and/or short action sequences. Number keys produce notes, both as sounds and pictured on the screen.

Documentation: Instructions and short descriptions of the response to each key.

Cataloging: 411   Alphabet

Publisher: Dynacomp, Inc.

Recommended: Classroom Computer News   March/April 1982
             Compute!   May 1982
             InfoWorld   November 30, 1981

HOMONYMS IN CONTEXT

Apple, TRS-80   Language Arts

Practice in selecting the correct homonym from the pairs presented in six different lessons, each with 25 sentences. Items missed are reviewed at the end of each lesson and the review is followed by a short game as a reward.

Documentation: Teacher's manual.

Cataloging: 423   English language - Homonyms

Publisher: Random House

Recommended: Electronic Learning   Mar/Apr 1982
             Electronic Learning   May/June 1982

IDEAL GAS LAW

Apple   Science

User controls pressure, volume, temperature, and the number of moles of gas in a container in order to observe the effects of changing one or more of the variables. Simulation is based on the kinetic-molecular theory of gases.

Documentation: Teacher's manual with instructions for use, student exercises, and study guide.

Cataloging: 530.7   Physics - Experiments

Publisher: High Technology, Inc. (Chem Lab Simulations 2)

Recommended: Creative Computing   September 1980
             InfoWorld   October 13, 1980

Apple   Logic

The maze is seen from inside, with the walls appearing as they would to a rat trying to run the maze. Students must try to work their way to the end.

Documentation: Instructions.

Cataloging: 793.7   Puzzles

Publisher: SoftSide

INTERVAL MANIA

Apple   Music

Practice in identifying melodic and harmonic intervals both visually and aurally is presented in game format. A basic knowledge of music notation and interval construction is a prerequisite.

Documentation: User's guide, data sheet, teacher's guide with instructions for setting difficulty levels and other parameters.

Cataloging: 780.7   Music - Study and teaching

Publisher: Micro Music Inc. (MMI)

Recommended: JEM Reference Manual   Vol. I   Release II
                    Journal of Courseware Review   Vol. 1   No. 1

JUGGLES' RAINBOW

Apple, Atari   Primary

Playful color animations introduce spatial concepts of right/left and above/below and provide a delightful introduction to the computer for the pre-reader.

Documentation: Child's story guide to the program, activity card.

Cataloging: 793.7   Puzzles

Publisher: The Learning Company

Recommended: Compute!   May 1982
                    Courseware Report Card   September 1982
                    CUE Newsletter   October 23, 1981
                    USER'S   November 1982

TRS-80   Math

Part I has testing and skill-building lessons for K-3. Part II has addition, sub-traction, multiplication, and division for grades 1-8 in three modes: placement, skill-building, and testing. Automatically advances student to harder or easier material in response to performance and prints out reports of student progress and test scores.

Documentation: Teacher's manual with objectives, instructions for use, sample problem pages, and student materials. The K-8 Math Cross-Reference Guide correlates the series with arithmetic basal texts. A K-8 math worksheet generator is available as a separate program to print out additional exercises.

Cataloging: 513   Arithmetic

Publisher: Radio Shack

Recommended: Arithmetic Teacher   September 1981
Creative Computing   October 1980
80 Microcomputing   February 1981
Electronic Learning   November/December 1981
EPIE Report   98/99m
MACUL Journal   Winter 1981

THE KAREL SIMULATOR

Apple   Computer Science

Karel the Robot introduces advanced students to structured programming by using a carefully adapted Pascal that contains no data structures. Karel can be programmed to jump hurdles, escape from mazes, and make other moves within a grid on the screen.

Documentation: Manual with very complete operating instructions comes with the program. Users will need to purchase KAREL THE ROBOT written by Karel's developer, Richard Pattis, and published by John Wiley & Sons.

Cataloging: 001.6   Programming (Electronic computers)

Publisher: Cybertronics International, Inc.

Recommended: Creative Computing   April 1982
CUE Newsletter   May 1982
Electronic Learning   September 1982
InfoWorld   April 26, 1982
The Computing Teacher   November 1981

PET   Computer Science

This version of Turtle Graphics introduces computer programming to novices and also provides a friendly introduction to the computer. Pictures and sound are easily created using the short list of simple commands.

Documentation: Detailed manual describes all features and commands of the language and all procedures; includes suggestions for use, classroom activities, and student exercises.

Cataloging: 400.28   Programming languages (Electronic computers)

Publisher: J.L. Hammett Company

Recommended: CUE Newsletter   August 15, 1982
             Educational Computer   November/December 1982
             Electronic Learning   September 1982
             Hands On!   Spring 1982
             InfoWorld   May 31, 1982
             School Microware Reviews   Summer 1982

KINGDOM

TRS-80   Social Studies

Ruler controls the population, agriculture, and economy of an ancient kingdom in this Hammurabi-type simulation.

Documentation: Instructions.

Cataloging: 338.9   Economic policy

Publisher: Micro Learningware (Educational Package II)

LEARNING BOX

Apple   Teacher Utility

Tic-tac-toe game format offers option of games with 3, 4 or 5 items across in each row. Students and teachers construct lists of questions and insert the answers into the program. Partners take turns reading the questions or spelling words and entering answers into the Tic Tac Toe game. The computer checks the answers and provides the game format motivation.

Documentation: Instructions for using the program and for entering new questions and answers.

Cataloging: 371.3   Authoring systems

Publisher: M.D. Fullmer & Associates

PET   Primary

Keyboard practice in matching oversize numbers and letters on the screen with the computer keyboard. Teacher can set upper or lower case, the numer of letters/numbers in each set, the number of sets, and whether to match or to fill the blanks in an alphabetical or numerical sequence.

Documentation: Teacher's guide and instructions.

Cataloging: 411   Alphabet

Publisher: Teaching Tools: Microcomputer Services

Recommended: Booklist   April 1, 1982
              Compute!   May 1982
              Creative Computing   February 1982
              Kilobaud Microcomputing   June 1981
              School Microware Reviews   Winter 1982

LINEAR SEARCH GAMES

Apple, PET, TRS-80   Math

Problem solving skills are developed through the use of a sequence of increasingly difficult games utilizing number lines.

Documentation: Teacher's guide includes objectives, program descriptions, instructions, suggestions for classroom use, and student activity sheets.

Cataloging: 411   Arithmetic

Publisher: Creative Publications

Recommended: Arithmetic Teacher   September 1981

MAGIC SPELLS

Apple   Language Arts

Students unscramble words to win gold and other treasure from the Spelling Demon. Help is always available, but the treasure won decreases in response to incorrect answers and the amount of help requested. Students and teachers can create their own word lists or use lists already in the program.

Documentation: Teacher's guide and instructions for entering individualized word lists.

Cataloging: 421   Engligh language - Spelling

Publisher: Apple Computer, Inc.

Recommended: Courseware Report Card   September 1982
CUE Newsletter   January 15, 1982

MARKET

Apple, TRS-80   Social Studies

Economic simulation has two users competing for profit in a bicycle manufacturing business. Advertising, production rate, costs, and sales price are determined by each player.

Documentation: Instructions.

Cataloging: 380.1   Marketing

Publisher: Creative Computing (Social & Economic Simulations)

Recommended: Creative Computing   April 1982

MASTERTYPE

Apple, Atari   Business Education

17 timed typing lessons have a graduated difficulty range from 3 letter combinations to 9 letter words, numerals and symbols. Arcade game format encourages students to learn touch typing and to improve their speed. Students and teachers may enter their own words into the games.

Documentation: Instruction manual.

Cataloging: 652.3   Typewriting

Publisher: Lightning Software

Recommended: Apple Journal of Courseware Review   Issue 1
Booklist   September 1, 1982
Classroom Computer News   January/February 1982
Courseware Report Card   September 1982
Creative Computing   April 1982
Electronic Learning   March/April 1982
InfoWorld   July 6, 1981
Softalk   April 1981
School Microware Reviews   Winter 1982

MATCH GAME

Apple, Atari, PET, TRS-80   Teacher Utility

Students or teachers can enter new data into the concentration type game format, choosing either exact matches or paired matches (math problem paired with its answer, English-Spanish word pairs, etc.). One to four players can play with or without the computer as a player. Size of game board varies from 2 to 10 matches. A dozen math and language arts games are already in the program.

Documentation: Suggested classroom uses and instructions for playing the game and for entering new data.

Cataloging: 793.7   Puzzles

Publisher: Teaching Tools: Microcomputer Services

Recommended: Creative Computing   February 1982
Kilobaud Micromputing   June 1981
School Microware Reviews   Winter 1982

MATH MACHINE

Apple   Math

There are 111 skill levels in this K-6 arithmetic drill package. Reinforcement is provided by the choice of one of six arcade-type games which run for one minute each time the student achieves a success level that is set by the teacher for each individual student.

Documentation: Teacher's manual with goals and objectives, suggested classroom activities and instructions for using the program.

Cataloging: 513   Arithmetic

Publisher: SouthWest EdPsych Services

Recommended: The Computing Teacher   December 1981
Creative Computing   October 1981
Instructor   October 1981
JEM Reference Manual   Vol. I   Release II
Micro-Scope   September 1981
School Microware Reviews   Winter 1982

MATH SEQUENCES

Apple, Atari, PET, TRS-80   Math

Drill in number readiness, addition, subtraction, multiplication, division, fractions, decimals, per cent, equations, and measurements, with provision for an instructional management system (Apple and Atari versions only) if desired. Students are automatically advanced to more difficult levels as they exhibit mastery.

Documentation: Teacher's guide, instructions, resources, sample program output, student record sheets, and a key that relates the program segments to standard math textbooks.

Cataloging: 513 Arithmetic

Publisher: Milliken Publishing Company

Recommended: Arithmetic Teacher   September 1981
      Booklist   October 1, 1981
      Book Report   September/October 1982
      Classroom Computer News   September/October 1981
      The Computing Teacher   September 1981
      Creative Computing   September 1980
      CUE Newsletter   August 15, 1981
      Educational Technology   October 1981
      Electronic Learning   September/October 1981
      EPIE Report   98/99m
      JEM Reference Manual   Vol. I   Release II
      Journal of Courseware Review   Vol. 1 No. 1
      Media & Methods   October 1981
      Micro-Scope   December 1980
      MicroSIFT   October 1981
      USER'S   March 1981

MATHEMATICS EDU-DISKS

Apple, TRS-80 Math

Highly interactive program individualizes basic math problems according to student's responses. The pre-test, practice, and post-test for each segment is administered to the student automatically and entered into the management system. A separate set of disks is available for each grade level, 1 through 7, with content correlated to ten basal math series.

Documentation: Teacher's guide, student workbook, and teacher's edition of the workbook.

Cataloging: 513 Arithmetic

Publisher: Reader's Digest

MICROCOMPUTER KEYBOARDING

Apple Business Education

Well-paced typing drill on correct finger positions does not allow student to continue until each sequence has been typed several times without error.

Documentation: Instruction manual.

Cataloging: 652.3 Typewriting

Publisher: South-Western Publishing Company

Apple, Atari, TRS-80   Computer Science

An introductory computer literacy program for grades 4-8. Presents the computer, programming concepts, and computer applications through the use of simulations.

Documentation: Student workbook, teacher's guide with lesson plans and suggested resources.

Cataloging: 621.3819   Computer Literacy

Publisher: Science Research Associates

MICRO-PAINTER

Apple, Atari   Art

Hi-res illustration tool that allows the user to draw shapes and then fill in each outlined area with any of up to 21 different colors.

Documentation: Complete illustrated instructions.

Cataloging: 702.8   Art - Technique

Publisher: Datasoft, Inc.

Recommended: Atari Computer Enthusiasts   July 1982
             INFOWORLD   July 26, 1982
             Softalk   April 1981

MILLIKAN EXPERIMENT, VERSION 2

PET   Science

Simulation of the Millikan Oil Drop Experiment uses the computer to replace a sometimes dangerous and expensive physics experiment for high school and college students.

Documentation: Instructions.

Cataloging: 530.7   Physics - Experiments

Publisher: Merlan Scientific

Recommended: Electronic Learning   September/October 1981

MOPTOWN

Apple   Logic

Moptown creatures are identified by four attributes (tall/short, fat/thin, red/blue, gribbit/bibbit) in a series of logic puzzle games that progress from preschool to adult difficulty levels. Students are challenged to use careful visual discrimination and high-level problem solving skills.

Documentation: Teacher's manual with suggested classroom activities.

Cataloging: 793.7   Puzzles

Publisher: Apple Computer, Inc.

Recommended: Booklist   September 1, 1982
Book Report   September/October 1982
Classroom Computer News   November/December 1982
CUE Newsletter   January 15, 1982
Electronic Learning   November 1982
School Microware Reviews   Summer 1982
Softalk   October 1982

Music!

PET   Music

Computer keys represent notes that, when pressed, produce a tone and a note shown on the staff on the screen. Type of note is determined by length of time key is held down. Tunes can be created, played, edited, and saved on tape or disk.

Documentation: Instructions.

Cataloging: 780.7   Music - Study and teaching

Publisher: CURSOR (#20   May 1980)

Recommended: Compute!   May 1982

Music: Terms & Notation

Atari   Music

Programs on disk: Introduction, Enharmonics, Key signature, Name the note, Terms, Note types.

Documentation: Teacher's manual and student activities.

Cataloging: 781   Music - Theory

Publisher: MECC

Music Theory

Apple   Music

Programs on disk: Introduction, Aural interval, Counting, Enharmonics, Find the half, Key signatures, Missing note, Name the note, Note types, Rhythm, Rhythm play, Scales, Sevenths, Terms, Triads, Visual intervals, Whole half, Wrong note.

Documentation: Teacher's manual and student activities.

Cataloging: 781   Music - Theory

Publisher: Apple Computer, Inc.
           MECC (available from MECC in Minnesota only)

Recommended: Electronic Learning   September/October 1981
                  JEM Reference Manual   Vol. I   Release II
                  Softalk   March 1981

My Telephone

PET   Primary

Names and telephone numbers can be entered for one child or for an entire class. When a child enters his or her name the telephone number appears on the screen with random digits left out. Child first enters missing digits and then types entire telephone number to receive a visual reward of a ringing phone.

Documentation: Very simple data entry instructions for teacher.

Cataloging: 372   Education, Elementary

Publisher: Educational Software Associates

Nine Games for Preschoolers

TRS-80   Primary

Six language alphabet games, a maze, and two math counting games can all be loaded into memory simultaneously and called from a master menu that does not require any reading skill. Varied graphics appeal to younger children.

Documentation: Instructions.

Cataloging: 793.7   Puzzles

Publisher: The Software Exchange

Recommended: Chicatrug News   October 1980
                  Creative Computing   August 1981
                  Creative Computing   October 1981

Number Line

Apple, Atari   Math

Addition and subtraction of positive and negative numbers is demonstrated on a number line using a moving arrow and flashing numbers. Student can choose addition, subtraction, or mixed randomly generated problems. Prompts user after second wrong answer.

Documentation: Teacher's guide with suggested student activities.

Cataloging: 513   Arithmetic

Publisher: EduSoft

Numeric Data Entry Practice Program

TRS-80   Business Education

Gives students practice in entering data using the numeric keypad of the TRS-80, with emphasis on both speed and accuracy.

Documentation: Teacher's manual with instructions for using the management package to maintain student records.

Cataloging: 650.7   Business Education

Publisher: Radio Shack

Odell Lake

Apple, Atari   Science

Students are introduced to food chains by simulating the behavior of fish in Odell Lake. Effective graphics provide immediate feedback on the results of student decisions.

Documentation: Teacher's guide includes objectives, operating instructions, suggested activities, program listing, student worksheets.

Cataloging: 574.5   Ecology

Publisher: MECC (Apple: Science Vol. 3 & Elementary Vol. 4; Atari: Elementary Biology)

Recommended: Apple Journal of Courseware Review   Issue 1
JEM Reference Manual   Vol. I   Release II
Journal of Courseware Review   Vol. 1 No. 1
MACUL Journal   Winter 1981
The Computing Teacher   April/May 1980
Purser's Magazine   Winter 1981
The Computing Teacher   April/May 1980

Apple, Atari   Social Studies

Students embark in a covered wagon on the trip from Missouri to Oregon in the 1800s. The challenge is to select supplies wisely and to make successful decisions in response to accidents and dangers along the trail. Students' determination to survive leads to a high degree of involvement and interaction.

Documentation: Teacher's guide with instructions, background information, classroom activities, bibliography, printout of sample run.

Cataloging: 978   Oregon Trail

Publisher: MECC (Apple: Elementary Vol. 6; Atari: American History)

Recommended: Electronic Learning   September/October 1981
                     Journal of Courseware Review   Vol. 1 No. 1
                     Softalk   May 1981

PAINT

Atari   Art

Developed at the Capital Children's Museum, this program encourages students to create pictures on the computer screen using many different colors, patterns, and techniques.

Documentation: Instruction manual provides detailed background information and guides students to explore the artistic creative potential of the computer.

Cataloging: 702.8   Art - Technique

Publisher: Reston Publishing Company

Recommended: Electronic Learning   October 1982
                     Media & Methods   May/June 1982
                     School Library Journal   August 1982
                     Softside   September 1982

PARTS OF SPEECH

Apple   Language Arts

Lessons and diagnostic drills on nouns, pronouns, adjectives, adverbs, verbs, interjections, and conjunctions.

Documentation: Student worksheets, teacher's guide with suggestions for classroom use, instructions for creating tests, and list of sentences used in program.

Cataloging: 425   English language - Grammar

Publisher: MECC (English Vol. 1)

Apple   Science

Ecological simulation that allows students to explore the environmental effects of pesticides.

Documentation: Teacher's manual and student activities.

Cataloging: 574.5   Ecology

Publisher: MECC (Science Vol. 2)

Recommended: JEM Reference Manual   Vol. I   Release II
                     MACUL Journal   Winter 1981

PHONICS

Atari   Reading

Sound on cassette combines with the computer in a unique and highly interactive series of nine lesson sequences on basic phonics elements.

Documentation: Teacher's manual with instructions and activities, student workbook.

Cataloging: 414   Phonetics

Publisher: Science Research Associates

PLOT

Apple, Atari, TRS-80   Math

Displays graphs of equations, conic sections, and trigonometric, exponential, or logarithmic functions. Two functions may be graphed and displayed on the screen at once, and plotting time is very fast. Recommended for algebra, analytic geometry, trig, and calculus.

Documentation: Teacher's guide.

Cataloging: 510   Mathematics

Publisher: EduSoft

Recommended: Creative Computing   September 1980
                     The Computing Teacher   Vol. 8 No. 6

PRACTICANDO ESPANOL CON LA MANZANA II

Apple   Foreign Language

Beginning and intermediate-level drills in Spanish verb conjugation and vocabulary (words and phrases). Teacher can add or delete verbs and vocabulary entries. Items are presented in random order and those that are missed are repeated. Errors are identified as either "accent" or "spelling" errors. Review and Help screens are available as needed.

Documentation: Instructor's Guide with directions for changing the drills, catalog of program contents, student information sheets, and instructions for using the management system.

Cataloging: 460.7   Spanish language - Study and teaching

Publisher: CONDUIT

Recommended: Journal of Courseware Review   Vol. 1 No. 1

PROBLEM SOLVING EDU-DISKS

Apple, TRS-80   Math

Solutions to word problems are developed using logical thinking and problem solving methods on the screen and in the accompanying student workbook. Students are helped to identify all of the important information in the problem as part of their strategy. Highly interactive.

Documentation: Teacher's Guide, student workbooks.

Cataloging: 513   Arithmetic

Publisher: Reader's Digest

PUNCTUATION SKILLS

Apple   Language Arts

Rules for ending punctuation marks, commas, colons, and semi-colons are explained and illustrated. Students are then challenged to complete the practice exercises correctly.

Documentation: Teacher's guide, ditto masters for student worksheets.

Cataloging: 421   Punctuation

Publisher: Milton Bradley

Recommended: Educational Technology   July 1982

QUICK QUIZ

TRS-80   Teacher Utility

Teachers use the framework provided to develop multiple-choice instructional activities for any subject area. Exercises and tests can be done on the computer or printed out for classroom use. Up to 50 separate student scores can be stored on the disk and/or printed out.

Documentation: Teacher's manual and instructions.

Cataloging: 371.3 Authoring systems

Publisher: Radio Shack

RATRUN

PET   Logic

Students see and run the maze from the perspective of the rat, turning and moving in any direction to reach the reward at the end.

Documentation: Instructions.

Cataloging: 793.7 Puzzles

Publisher: CURSOR (#13 August/September 1979)

READABILITY ANALYSIS PROGRAM

Apple, TRS-80   Teacher Utility

A readability index based upon the most widely-used formulas—Flesch, Fog, Dale-Chall and Smog (plus Wheeler-Smith and Spache in the Apple version)— calculates reading level for passages typed into the computer. Can print either a simple summary reading level or a detailed analysis of the passage.

Documentation: Teacher's manual includes instructions for use, directions for printing both passages and reading levels, explanation and worksheet for each of the formulas.

Cataloging: 372.4 Reading

Publisher: Random House

Recommended: Educational Technology April 1982

READING LEVEL

Apple, PET, TRS-80   Teacher Utility

Selections of approximately 100 words at a time are analyzed for grade level based on Bormuth's Readability Formula. Groups of words can also be analyzed for grade level and be displayed or printed in alphabetical order, in order by word length or in order by number of syllables.

Documentation: Teacher's guide with objectives and directions for using the program, a sample run and program listing, references and summary worksheets.

Cataloging: 372.4   Reading

Publisher: School CourseWare Journal   (September 1981)

Sammy, the Sea Serpent

Atari   Primary

Sammy's adventures are told via a tape recorder while the child uses the joystick to play games with Sammy, guide him through a maze and participate in other adventures.

Documentation: Instructions.

Cataloging: 793.7   Puzzles

Publisher: Program Design, Inc.

Recommended: Creative Computing   October 1981
             Microcomputing   October 1982
             Purser's Atari Magazine   Fall 1981

Scatter

Apple, PET, TRS-80   Science

Physics demonstration in which students must determine the shape of various objects placed in the path of a moving particle based upon observation of the new path that the particle takes when it is deflected. There are three levels of difficulty.

Documentation: Teacher's guide with examples and diagrams of the activity, references, instructions for program modification, student activities, and questions. Student guide.

Cataloging: 530.7   Physics - Experiments

Publisher: CONDUIT

Recommended: Journal of Courseware Review   Vol. 1 No. 1
             Purser's Magazine   Summer 1980

Scram

Atari   Science

Simulation of an atomic reactor melt-down. Students make decisions regarding various hazards, safety precautions and reactions to each situation as it develops.

Documentation: Complete instructions and background information.

Cataloging: 621.48   Atomic power plants

Publisher: Atari

Recommended: Purser's Atari Magazine   Fall 1981

SCREEN PRO 40

PET   Language Arts

Very simple text editor allows user to create a screen of text and/or graphics and save the screen on tape or disk. One screen at a time can be recalled for editing using the cursor keys, and screen can also be printed. User-friendly program with applications for students and teachers.

Documentation: Instruction manual.

Cataloging: 808   English language - Composition and exercises

Publisher: Educational Software Associates

SEARCH

PET   Language Arts

Produces a word search puzzle with up to 25 words selected by the teacher or student. Puzzle is randomly generated and will be different each time, even using the same words. User can watch the screen to see the computer trying to place words into the puzzle. Prints answer key and then prints puzzle.

Documentation: Instructions in program. Printer needed.

Cataloging: 793.7   Word games

Publisher: CURSOR (#14   October 1979)

SELL LEMONADE

Apple, Atari   Social Studies

Business simulation in game format introduces economic concepts and provides math practice. Users try to make a profit selling lemonade by determining quantities, costs, and advertising based on weather forecasts.

Documentation: Instruction manual, teacher's guide, student worksheets.

Cataloging: 380.1   Marketing

Publisher: MECC (Apple: Elementary Vol. 3; Atari: The Market Place)

Recommended: Creative Computing   April 1982
MACUL Journal   Winter 1981
Peelings II   January 1982

SENTENCE DIAGRAMMING

Apple   Language Arts

Grammatical usage, parts of speech, sentence types, and sentence diagramming for high school students, with series of 20 sentences in each of three difficulty levels. Disk has optional record keeping function.

Documentation: Teacher's manual with detailed instructions.

Cataloging: 425   English language - Grammar

Publisher: Avant-Garde Creations

Recommended: Apple Journal of Courseware Review   Issue 1
The Computing Teacher   Vol. 8   No. 7
Creative Computing   October 1981
InfoWorld   November 23, 1981
Journal of Courseware Review   Vol. 1 No. 2
Peelings II   March/April 1981

SHELL GAMES

Apple   Teacher Utility

Teacher-created quiz can be set up as matching, true-false or multiple choice questions and entered into one of the three game formats.

Documentation: Operating instructions for teachers and students are listed in the program. The teacher's manual has instructional objectives, operating instructions, follow-up activities and a bibliography.

Cataloging: 371.3   Authoring systems

Publisher: Apple Computer, Inc.

Recommended: Journal of Learning Disabilities   June/July 1982
MicroSIFT   December 1981
Purser's Magazine   Fall 1981
School Library Journal   August 1982

SNARK

Apple, Atari   Math

Students search for the Snark hidden in a 10 x 10 grid in this game-formatted introduction to coordinate geometry. The Snark can be trapped by entering X and Y coordinates and the radius of the circle to be drawn from that point. The computer then tells whether the Snark is inside, outside or on the circle.

Documentation: Teacher's manual and suggested student activities.

Cataloging: 516   Geometry

Publisher: MECC (Apple: Mathematics, Vol. 1; Atari: Graphing)

Recommended: JEM Reference Manual   Vol. I   Release II
MACUL Journal   Winter 1981

SPANISH HANGMAN

Apple   Foreign Language

This Spanish/English Hangman game has 1600 words and 450 sentences. Student can choose English or Spanish at several levels of difficulty. French version is also available.

Documentation: Instructions.

Cataloging: 460.7   Spanish language - Study and teaching

Publisher: George Earl

Recommended: The Computing Teacher   Vol. 8 No. 4
Microcomputers in Education   January 1981
Peelings   November/December 1980
Purser's Magazine   Winter 1981
School Microware Reviews   Winter 1982
School Microware Reviews   Summer 1982

SPELLING PACKAGE

Apple, PET   Language Arts

Teacher dictates up to 50 words into an audio cassette recorder and enters the same words into the computer. Package includes a tape recorder interface card that allows the computer to turn the audio cassette on and off when student presses the Return key to hear one dictated word at a time. Student enters the word into the computer and teachers can choose to have errors handled by: asking student to try again, printing the correct letters on the screen and ask the student to try again, or showing correct spelling and have student type the word correctly.

Documentation: Teacher's guide with instructions for entering any type of individualized word list and for operating the program.

Cataloging: 421   English language - Spelling

Publisher: Teaching Tools: Microcomputer Services

Recommended: Creative Computing   February 1982
Electronic Learning   November/December 1981
Peelings   November/December 1980
School Microware Reviews   Winter 1982

SPELL 'N' TIME

Apple, PET, TRS-80   Language Arts

Speed drill on spelling words selected by the teacher from any subject area and at any grade level. A single word is flashed on the screen, with time varying according to student performance. The student types the word after it disappears. Incorrect words are flashed in syllables and repeated.

Documentation: Excellent teacher's guide includes a sample program run, listing, instructions for modifying the program, word lists, educational objectives, and related activities.

Cataloging: English language - Spelling

Publisher: School CourseWare Journal (September 1980)

Recommended: Byte   November 1981
Purser's Magazine   Winter 1981
School Microware Reviews   Summer 1981

SUMER

Apple   Social Studies

Students rule the ancient kingdom of Sumer and attempt to make decisions that will allow the citizens to prosper.

Documentation: Student activity sheets, teacher's guide, background information and suggested classroom activities.

Cataloging: 338.9   Economic policy

Publisher: MECC (Elementary Vol. 6)

Recommended: MACUL Journal   Winter 1981

TAG

Apple, Atari, Pet, TRS-80   Science

User estimates the bass population in a pond where the fish are tagged for identification, simulating a wildlife management study.

Documentation: Instructions, student manual.

Cataloging: 639   Wildlife - Conservation

Publisher: Creative Computing (Ecology Simulations I)

Recommended: MACUL Journal   Spring 1980

THREE MILE ISLAND

Apple   Science

Student controls activation of turbines, pumps, valves, filters, etc., in a nuclear power facility. The simulated operation can lead to a melt-down if not handled properly.

Documentation: Detailed description of atomic reactor operation, diagrams and program instructions.

Cataloging: 621.48   Atomic power plants

Publisher: Muse Software

Recommended: The Computing Teacher   Vol. 8 No. 2
Purser's Magazine   Spring 1980
SoftSide   July 1980

TITRATE

PET   Science

Simulation of titration process which allows user to control amount and speed of chemical being added. Student learns the scientific concept and receives practice in performing the process of titration.

Documentation: Short notes.

Cataloging: 540.7   Chemistry - Experiments

Publisher: CURSOR (#10   May 1979)

Recommended: MACUL Journal   Spring 1980

TOUCH TYPING

Atari   Business Education

Introduction to the keyboard and practice with correct fingering techniques.

Documentation: Instruction manual.

Cataloging: 652.3   Typewriting

Publisher: Atari

TRS-80   Computer Science

COLOR LOGO is a computer language for children. It uses Turtle Graphics with multiple turtles to encourage them to explore the computer and to become actively involved in the learning process. Very young children can use the program to produce simple patterns on the screen.

Documentation: Teacher's manual, complete instructions, sample programs, and guide to the programming techniques.

Cataloging: 400.28   Programming languages (Electronic computers)

Publisher: Radio Shack

TRS-80 MicroPILOT

TRS-80   Teacher Utility

Flexible, command-oriented author language based on PILOT, with added graphics and file handling capability. Teachers can create instructional materials in any subject area.

Documentation: Teacher's manual and instructions, sample lesson and user's Reference Card.

Cataloging: 400.28   Programming languages (Electronic computers)

Publisher: Radio Shack

Recommended: Electronic Learning   January/February 1982

TYPING TUTOR II

Apple, TRS-80   Business Education

Traditional typing course to teach keyboard and typing skills. Section I is a tutorial and Section II has timed and graded practice exercises. Constant feedback on speed and accuracy analyzes errors and shows keys missed.

Documentation: Instruction manual.

Cataloging: 652.3   Typewriting

Publisher: Microsoft

Recommended: Apple Journal of Courseware Review   Issue 1
              Educational Technology   October 1981
              80 Microcomputing   February 1981
              Purser's Magazine   Fall 1981
              School Microware Reviews   Summer 1981
              School Microware Reviews   Summer 1982

VOYAGEUR

Apple   Social Studies

Historic simulation of a fur trading expedition via canoe across Minnesota and Ontario during the early 1800s. Students select supplies for the trip, make trading decisions, respond to various hazards and problems along the way.

Documentation: Teacher's guide, objectives, instructions, student worksheets and suggested activities.

Cataloging: 338.3   Fur trade - History

Publisher: MECC (Elementary Vol. 6)

WORD PUZZLE

TRS-80   Language Arts

User can enter up to 16 words and computer develops a square grid of letters with words hidden within it vertically, horizontally, diagonally, and backwards. Puzzle appears on screen and also can be printed. List of hidden words appears beside the puzzle.

Documentation: Instructions in program.

Cataloging: 793.7   Word games

Publisher: CLOAD Magazine Inc.   (March 1982)

SECTION **VI**

Appendixes and Indexes

Appendix A

Copyright Regulations

The legal copying of commercial software is governed by the 1976 Copyright Reform Act. Public Law 96-517, December 12, 1980, amends Section 117 of Title 17 of the 1976 Copyright Reform Act to read as follows:

117. Limitations on exclusive rights: Computer programs

Notwithstanding the provisions of section 106, it is not an infringement for the owner of a copy of a computer program to make or authorize the making of another copy or adaptation of that computer program provided:

(1) that such a new copy or adaptation is created as an essential step in the utilization of the computer program in conjunction with a machine and that it is used in no other manner, or

(2) that such new copy or adaptation is for archival purposes only and that all archival copies are destroyed in the event that continued possession of the computer program should cease to be rightful.

Any exact copies prepared in accordance with the provisions of this section may be leased, sold, or otherwise transferred, along with the copy from which such copies were prepared, only as part of the lease, sale, or other transfer of all rights in the program. Adaptations so prepared may be transferred only with the authorization of the copyright owner.

The language of the law thus specifically limits the copying of copyrighted computer programs to use "FOR ARCHIVAL PURPOSES ONLY" and forbids all other copying unless authorized by the copyright owner. A rough but useful guideline is to examine WHY any duplicate copy is being made. Backup copies that are used only if the original software is damaged appear to be legal. Illegal copies are those made to avoid the cost of purchasing duplicate programs for use on other microcomputers or in other classrooms.

It is useful to have two separate courseware collections, one for users and another for the backup copies. One backup copy should be made when the software is purchased if this is possible. Some publishers copylock their software but will sell backup copies at a discount when the original purchase is made. Other publishers offer license agreements to allow the user to reproduce the courseware for a stated number of computers, classrooms or schools. Leasing courseware is another option being offered by a few publishers; depending upon the publisher's policy, this may provide the advantage of making new editions of the courseware available at little or no additional cost.

Backup copies, with copies of all documentation, need to be stored in a locked or otherwise secure area that can be accessed by only one or two persons. They should be used only when the originals are damaged and must be replaced.

The entire issue of courseware duplication and copyright protection is a controversial one in the field of educational computing. Publishers frequently feel that they are being cheated by teachers who make illegal copies of their courseware. Teachers may say "it's for the good of the students" or "courseware is too expensive" to try to justify illegal copying, not realizing what a poor example they are setting for their students. Publishers and teachers will hopefully begin to work together to develop courseware duplication policies that can meet instructional needs and still provide a fair return to the publishers on their investment.

Appendix **B**

Evaluation Guidelines

GUIDELINES FOR EVALUATING COMPUTERIZED INSTRUCTIONAL MATERIALS

Published by: National Council of Teachers of Mathematics
1906 Association Drive
Reston VA 22091
$3.75

The evaluation criteria in this booklet are well developed, with clear explanations and examples, and the evaluation forms are simple and easy to complete. They can be used effectively with courseware for any subject area and are especially recommended for the novice.

THE EVALUATOR'S GUIDE FOR MICROCOMPUTER-BASED INSTRUCTIONAL PACKAGES (MICROSIFT)

Published by: The Computing Teacher
Dept. of Computer & Information Science
Univeristy of Oregon
Eugene OR 97403
$2.50

This comprehensive evaluation document was designed to establish a model of excellence in courseware. It has been thoroughly field-tested as part of the

MicroSIFT project. The guidelines and forms are more complex than those from NCTM, but the user who studies them carefully will learn a great deal about evaluation. Courseware developers will find this publication especially helpful.

THE CALIFORNIA LIBRARY MEDIA CONSORTIUM FOR CLASSROOM EVALUATION OF MICROCOMPUTER COURSEWARE

The goal in creating this form was to encourage teachers to participate in the evaluation process by making it as short and simple as possible. It is designed to be presented to teachers at a workshop and there is no written documentation. Permission is granted to reproduce the form and to modify it as desired to meet local needs.

COURSEWARE REVIEW AND RATING FORM

This two page form was originally published in the December 1979/January 1980 issue of THE COMPUTING TEACHER and may be reproduced without further permission.

Authoring Guides

Two publications written for designers and programmers in the field of instructional computing are included here as valuable sources of more detailed information on the criteria used in evaluating as well as developing excellent courseware.

AUTHOR'S GUIDE: DESIGN, DEVELOPMENT, STYLE, PACKAGING, REVIEW. Harold J. Peters and James W. Johnson. CONDUIT 1978.

DESIGNING INSTRUCTIONAL COMPUTING MATERIALS FOR USE WITH THE APPLE II MICROCOMPUTER. MECC 1981.

THE COMPUTING TEACHER

COURSEWARE REVIEW AND RATING FORM
(These forms may be duplicated for your use)

Date _____   Computer package is used on_____

Name of program _____

Name of cassette (if different from the program) _____

_____ tape # _____

Manufacturer's or distributor's name _____

Author's name (if known) _____

Reviewer's name _____

1. *Abstract*

"COPY ME"

2. If you can, suggest the title of course(s) for which this material is appropriate. (For example: arithmetic, reading, business machines, physics, etc.)

3. Indicate the appropriate instructional level(s) for use of this package.

_____ primary   _____ elementary   _____ junior high   _____ senior high   _____ college

4. Please indicate prerequisite skills (or courses) required for student use of this package. (for example: requires ability to graph, skill in multiplication, knowledge of first year French vocabulary, etc.)

5. Describe the type of computer application(s) used in this package (check one or more).

____ *simulation* (a model which behaves like some portion of the real world)

____ *game* (the student takes partial or total control of one side of the action)

____ *drill and practice* (the computer acts as a drillmaster)

____ *tutorial* (the computer describes some concept or process and then engages the student in a question and answer dialog)

____ *problem solving* (the student learns about some aspect of the real world by writing or using a computer program to solve the problem)

____ *remediation*

____ *enrichment*

____ *other* (specify) _____

6. Is it reasonable to use the computer with this package to help teach/learn the material (or can you see a more efficient or effective method).

_____ yes   _____ no   _____ not sure
comment:

7. Does the package contain a "title and author frame" which introduces the package to the user?

_____ yes   _____ no   _____ not sure

–12–

Evaluation Guidelines / 165

8. Does the package include sufficient documentation (written materials telling when and how to use the material and backup and resource materials, and also instructions included in the program) to aid · teachers and students in using the package?

_____ yes   _____ no   . _____ not sure
comment:

9. Does the package make use of the motivational devices of:

Timing: _____ yes   _____ no   _____ not sure

Scoring: _____ yes   _____ no   _____ not sure
Graphics: (graphs, moving 'pictures', etc.)

        _____ yes   _____ no   _____ not sure
Personalization: (informal, conversational, addressing student by name, etc.)

        _____ yes   _____ no   _____ not sure

10. Identify the strengths and weaknesses of this package: **"COPY ME"**

COURSEWARE REVIEW AND RATING FORM

SUMMARY EVALUATION

1 Level of interest:

                very interesting   A   B   C   D   F   uninteresting

2. Ease of use:

                easy to use   A   B   C   D   F   awkward

3. Educational content and/or value:

                much   A   B   C   D   F   little

4. Program polish:

                well done   A   B   C   D   F   amateurish, sloppy,
                                                      incomplete

5. Instructions:

                very clear   A   B   C   D   F   none

6. Use of graphics:

                excellent use   A   B   C   D   F   no use

7. Program responds differently for good students and poor students!

    a great deal of difference   A   B   C   D   F   no difference is seen
                    is seen

8. Use of computer delivery:

    very effective, can't be done   A   B   C   D   F   there are better ways to
    as well by any other means   achieve this objective

OVERALL VALUE:

    every school should have   A   B   C   D   F   not worth the effort to
                this program   load it

Please provide a paragraph summarizing your reactions to the program. Include in your summary as much of the material as you can from question 2 on, or on back of this page.

CALIFORNIA LIBRARY
MEDIA CONSORTIUM FOR
CLASSROOM EVALUATION
OF MICROCOMPUTER COURSEWARE
1983
(Revised)

FOLD HERE AND STAPLE TO RETURN (ADDRESS ON REVERSE)

Program title _____
Title on package/diskette _____
Microcomputer(s) brand/model _____ Memory needed ___ _____ K
Language _____ BASIC (or __ _____) Version/copyright date _____ Cost _____
Publisher _____
Peripherals needed: _____ Disk drive(s) _ ___ Cassette ____ Printer (Other _____)
Other materials/equipment needed _____
Backup copy available? Yes _____ No ____ Network/Hard Disk Possible? Yes _____ No ____

★ ★

Reviewed by _____
Grade level/subject/position _____
School/District _____
Address/Phone _____
May we use your name in the published review? _____
THANK YOU FOR YOUR CONTRIBUTION! PLEASE RETURN IMMEDIATELY TO THE ADDRESS ON THE BACK.

PROGRAM TITLE: _____ _____ _____ SUBJECT AREAS: _____

SUGGESTED GRADE LEVELS (Circle) K 1 2 3 4 5 6 7 8 9 10 11 12 College Teacher-use
TYPE OF PROGRAM (Check all that apply):

___ authoring system	___demonstration	___logic, problem-solving	___tutorial
___business applications	___drill/practice	___simulation	___utility
___ classroom management	___educational game	___teachers' utility	___word processing
___database management	___game	___testing	___Other:_____

SCOPE: (Check one):
_____ one or more programs on single topic   _____ one program in an instructional series
_____ group of unrelated programs   _____ multi-disk curriculum package

EVALUATION CRITERIA

YES NO N/A   GENERAL DESIGN: ___EXCELLENT ___GOOD ___WEAK ___NOT ACCEPTABLE

___ ___ ___   1. Creative, innovative use of computer?
___ ___ ___   2. Effective, appropriate use of computer?
___ ___ ___   3. Follows sound instructional organization?
___ ___ ___   4. Fits well into the curriculum?
___ ___ ___   5. Free of programming errors, problems?

                CONTENT: ___EXCELLENT ___GOOD ___WEAK ___NOT ACCEPTABLE

___ ___ ___   6. Branches to easier or harder material in response to student performance?
___ ___ ___   7. Factually correct?
___ ___ ___   8. Free of excessive violence or competition?
___ ___ ___   9. Free of stereotypes - race, ethnic, gender, age, handicapped?
___ ___ ___   10. Interest, difficulty, typing, and vocabulary levels are appropriate?
___ ___ ___   11. Modifications of data, speed, word lists., etc., by instructor are possible?
___ ___ ___   12. Punctuation, spelling, grammar correct?
___ ___ ___   13. Responses to errors are helpful, avoiding sarcasm or scolding?
___ ___ ___   14. Responses to student success are positive, enjoyable and appropriate?

                EASE OF USE: ___EXCELLENT ___GOOD ___WEAK ___NOT ACCEPTABLE

___ ___ ___   15. Answers may be corrected by user before continuing with program?
___ ___ ___   16. Instructions within program are clear, complete, concise?
___ ___ ___   17. Instructions can be skipped or recalled to screen?
___ ___ ___   18. Instructions on how to end program, start over, are given?
___ ___ ___   19. Menu allows user to access specific parts of program?
___ ___ ___   20. Paging speed and sequence can be controlled by user?
___ ___ ___   21. Screens are neat, attractive, well-spaced?
___ ___ ___   22. Sound, if present, is appropriate and may be turned off?

MOTIVATIONAL DEVICES USED: ___EXCELLENT ___GOOD ___WEAK ___NOT ACCEPTABLE
(Check all which apply):

_____ graphics for instruction	_____ color	_____ game format	_____ sound _____ timing
_____ graphics for reward	_____ scoring	_____ random order	_____ personalization

DOCUMENTATION:
(Check all available):   ___ EXCELLENT ___GOOD ___WEAK ___NOT ACCEPTABLE

___none	___instructions appear on screen	___tests
___ instruction manual	___suggested classroom activities	___workbook
___ teacher's guide	___ instructional objectives	___student worksheets

OVERALL OPINION
___Great program. I recommend it highly!
___Pretty good, useful.
___OK, but you might wait for a better one.
___Would select only if modifications were made.
___Not useful.

INSTRUCTIONAL CONTENT AND OBJECTIVES
(PLEASE USE ADDITIONAL SHEETS IF NEEDED)

● Describe content and main objectives of this program:

   In your opinion, were the objectives met?
● What classroom management, testing, or performance reporting is provided?

   How many students/classes can be managed by this program?
   Is the management system easy to use?

● Describe any special strengths of program:

● Comments/concerns/questions:

● Comments comparing with other programs which are similar:

● Suggestions to author/publisher:

BRIEFLY DESCRIBE STUDENTS & THEIR RESPONSE TO PROGRAM

Grade level(s) where used: _____ Subject: _____
Behavior observed that indicates learning took place:

Other reactions:

Any problems experienced?

Any quotes you want to share?

Appendix C

Sources of Courseware Reviews

AEDS Bulletin
Association for Educational Data Systems
1201 Sixteenth Street, N.W.
Washington D.C. 20036

AEDS Monitor
Association for Educational Data Systems
1201 Sixteenth Street, N.W.
Washington D.C. 20036

Classroom Computer News
Box 266
Cambridge MA 02138

Educational Computer
Box 535
Cupertino CA 95015

Electronic Education
1311 Executive Center Drive   Suite 220
Tallahassee FL 32301

Electronic Learning
902 Sylvan Avenue
Englewood Cliffs NJ 07632

**Journal of Computers in Mathematics
& Science Teaching**
Box 4455
Austin TX 78765

Microcomputers in Education
5 Chapel Hill Drive
Fairfield CT 06432

Micro-Scope
JEM Research
Discovery Park
University of Victoria
Box 1700
Victoria B.C. V8W 2Y2 Canada

The Computing Teacher
Dept. of Computer and Information
   Science
University of Oregon
Eugene OR 97403

Apple Journal of Courseware Review
Available from local dealer

Booklist
50 East Huron Street
Chicago IL 60611

The Book Report
Box 14466
Columbus OH 43214

Courseware Report Card
150 West Carob Street
Compton CA 90220

Digest of Software Reviews: Education
1341 Bulldog Lane Suite C
Fresno CA 93710

EPIE Micro-Courseware PRO/FILES
EPIE & Consumer's Union
Box 620
Stony Brook NY 11790

JEM Reference Manual
JEM Research
Discovery Park
University of Victoria
Box 1700
Victoria B.C. V8W 2Y2 Canada

Micro Media Review
Box 425
Ridgefield CT 06877

MicroSIFT Reviews
Northwest Regional Educational
    Laboratory
300 S.W. Sixth Avenue
Portland OR 97204

Peelings II (Apple)
945 Brook Circle
Las Cruces NM 88001

Purser's Atari Magazine (Atari)
Box 466
El Dorado CA 95623

Purser's Magazine
Box 466
El Dorado CA 95623

School Library Journal
Box 13706
Philadelphia PA 19101

School Microware Reviews
Dresden Associates
Box 246
Dresden ME 04342

NEWSLETTERS FROM EDUCATIONAL USERS' GROUPS

Atari Computer Enthusaists (Atari)
3662 Vine Maple Drive
Eugene OR 97405

Chicatrug News (TRS-80)
Chicago TRS-80 Users Group
203 N. Wabash Room 1510
Chicago IL 60601

CUE Newsletter
Computer-Using Educators
Box 18547
San Jose CA 95158

MACUL Journal
Michigan Association for Computer Users
in Learning
Wayne County ISD
33500 Van Born Avenue
Wayne MI 48184

**User's: The MECC Instructional
Computing Newsletter**
2520 North Broadway Drive
St. Paul MN 55113

Midnight Software Gazette   (PET)
Central Illinois PET Users' Group
635 Maple Court
Mt. Zion IL 62549

EDUCATION JOURNALS

Arithmetic Teacher
National Council of Teachers of
Mathematics
1906 Association Drive
Reston VA 22091

Educational Technology
140 Sylvan Avenue
Englewood Cliffs NJ 07632

Epie Report
Epie Institute
Box 620
Stony Brook NY 11790

Instructor
7 Bank Street
Dansville NY 14437

Journal of Learning Disabilities
5615 West Cermak Road
Cicero IL 60650

Mathematics Teacher
National Council of Teachers of
Mathematics
1906 Association Drive
Reston VA 22091

Media & Methods
1511 Walnut Street
Philadelphia PA 19102

COMPUTER JOURNALS

BYTE
70 Main Street
Peterborough NH 03458

Compute!
Box 5406
Greensboro NC 27403

Creative Computing
Box 789-M
Morristown NJ 07690

80 Microcomputing   (TRS-80)
80 Pine Street
Peterborough NH 03458

Infoworld
375 Cochituate Road
Box 880
Framingham MA 01701

Interface Age
16704 Marquardt Avenue
Cerritos CA 90701

Kilobaud Microcomputing
(see Microcomputing)

Microcomputing
80 Pine Street
Peterborough NH 03458

Nibble   (Apple)
Box 325
Lincoln MA 01773

onComputing
(see Popular Computing)

Personal Computing
50 Essex Street
Rochelle Park NJ 07662

Popular Computing
70 Main Street
Peterborough NH 03458

SoftSide
Box 68
Milford NH 03055

Softalk Magazine (Apple)
11021 Magnolia Boulevard
North Hollywood CA 91601

Courseware Directory Publishers

Apple Computer, Inc.
10260 Bandley Drive
Cupertino CA 95014

Atari
1265 Borregas Avenue
Sunnyvale CA 94086

Avant-Garde Creations
Box 30160
Eugene OR 97403

California School for the Deaf
39350 Gallaudet Drive
Fremont CA 94538

Chromasette
Box 1087
Santa Barbara CA 93102

CLOAD Magazine Inc.
Box 1448
Santa Barbara CA 93102

CompuPoem
S. Stephen Marcus
South Coast Writing Project
University of California
Santa Barbara CA 93106

Computer-Advanced Ideas, Inc.
1442A Walnut Street   Suite 341
Berkeley CA 94709

CONDUIT
Box 388
Iowa City IA 52244

CourseWare Magazine
(see School CourseWare Journal)

Creative Computing
Box 789-M
Morristown NJ 07960

Creative Publications
Box 10328
Palo Alto CA 94303

Curriculum Applications
16 Plymouth Street
Arlington MA 02174

CURSOR
The Code Works
Box 550
Goleta CA 93017

Cybertronics International, Inc.
Software Publishing Division
999 Mount Kemble Avenue
Morristown NJ 07960

Datasoft, Inc.
16606 Schoenborn Street
Sepulveda CA 91343

Dynacomp, Inc.
1427 Monroe Street
Rochester NY 1461

Educational Software Associates
5702 Genoa
Oakland CA 94608

Edu-Soft
4639 Spruce Street
Philadelphia PA 19139

George Earl
1302 South General McMullan
San Antonio TX 78237

Hartley Courseware, Inc.
Box 431
Dimondale MI 48821

Hayden Book Company, Inc.
50 Essex Street
Rochelle Park NJ 07662

High Technology, Inc.
Box 14665
Oklahoma City OK 73113

Ideatech Company
Box 62451
Sunnyvale CA 94088

Instant Software, Inc.
Peterborough NH 03458

J.L. Hammett Company
Box 545
Braintree MA 02184

L & S Computerware
1589 Fraser Drive
Sunnyvale CA 94087

The Learning Company   (TLC)
4370 Alpine Road
Portola Valley CA 94025

Lightning Software
Box 5223
Stanford CA 94305

M.D. Fullmer & Associates
1132 Via Jose   Suite D
San Jose CA 95120

Math Software
1233 Blackthorn Place
Deerfield IL 60015

McGraw-Hill Book Company
School Division
1221 Avenue of the Americas
New York NY 10020

MECC   (Minnesota Educational
    Computing Consortium)
2520 Broadway Drive
St. Paul MN 55113

Merlan Scientific
247 Armstrong Avenue   Unit 6
Georgetown, Ontario
Canada L7G 4X6

Microcomputers in Education
Robbinsdale Area Schools
4148 Winnetka Avenue North
Minneapolis MN 55427

MicroGnome Software
Fireside Computing, Inc.
5843 Montgomery Road
Elkridge MD 21227

Micro Learningware
Box 2134
North Mankato MN 56001

Micro Music Inc. (MMI)
390 Beaufort
Normal IL 61761

Microsoft Consumer Products
400 108th Avenue, N.E.
Bellevue WA 98004

Milliken Publishing Co.
1100 Research Blvd.
St. Louis MO 63132

Milton Bradley Company
443 Shaker Road
East Long Meadow MA 01101

Muse Software
330 N. Charles Street
Baltimore MD 21201

Program Design, Inc. (PDI)
11 Idar Court
Greenwich CT 06830

QED (Quality Educational Designs)
2924 N.E. Stanton
Portland OR 97212

Radio Shack
Education Division
1300 One Tandy Center
Ft. Worth TX 76102

Random House
School Division
Department 985   Suite 201
2970 Brandywine Road
Atlanta GA 30341

Reader's Digest
Educational Division
Pleasantville NY 10570

Reston Publishing Company
11480 Sunset Hills Road
Reston VA 22090

School CourseWare Journal
1341 Bulldog Lane   Suite C
Fresno CA 93710

Science Research Associates,
   Inc. (SRA)
155 North Wacker Drive
Chicago Il 60606

SoftSide
6 South Street
Milford NH 03055

Software Connections
1800 Wyatt Drive Suite 17
Santa Clara CA 95054

The Software Exchange
6 South Street
Milford NH 03055

Steketee Educational Software
(see Edu-Soft)

SouthWest EdPsych Services
Box 1870
Phoenix AZ 85001

South-Western Publishing Company
5101 Madison Road
Cincinnati OH 45227

Teaching Tools: Microcomputer
Services
Box 50065
Palo Alto CA 94303

Appendix E

Policies and Procedures for Selection of Instructional Materials

Policies and Procedures for Selection of Instructional Materials (1976) *is a revision of the former document approved by the Board of Directors of the American Association of School Librarians (AASL) at the ALA Midwinter Meeting in 1970. The following revision, which contains a model for the selection process, was adopted by the AASL Board of Directors on August 15, 1976. A statement of the American Association of School Librarians endorsing the* Library Bill of Rights *of the American Library Association is included within this document.*

I. INTRODUCTION

The human worth that democratic societies seek to protect and develop rests upon commitment to educational programs which meet the individual purposes and developmental needs of students and prepare them to resolve the problems that continually confront them. Social, economic, and political issues, national and international as well as the changing expectations of individuals and groups, represent the human concerns to which education must respond if it is to perpetuate and improve the society that supports it.

Those who would create better educational opportunities must strive to develop comprehensive systems that meet the needs of students of differing abilities, backgrounds, and interests, enabling them both to adjust to and influence the changing society in which they live. Media programs which reflect applications of educational technology, communication theory, and library and information science contribute at every level, offering essential processes, functions, and resources to accomplish the purposes of the school.[1]

Committed to the philosophy of school media programs as expressed in *Media Programs: District and School* and the selection of quality media collections which ensure that "learners will have the opportunity to grow in their ability to find, generate, evaluate, and apply information that helps them to function effectively as individuals and to participate fully in society," the American Association of School Librarians has prepared this material as a guide for the formulation of selection policies and procedures for the school media program.

The selection of quality instructional materials is one of the most important and controversial tasks performed by school personnel. Often school districts are subject to challenge by individuals or groups who are concerned about what the collection does or does not include. Such action may be based on considerations involving political, social, or personal values, religion, profanity, treatment of matters relating to sex, or other controversial issues.

A selection policy, therefore, should provide a procedure for maintaining a consistent quality of excellence in the materials for use in the teaching-learning process including continuing evaluation of the media collection. The American Association of School Librarians *believes* that such a policy and procedures statement should be adopted formally and approved officially by each school district as a basis for selecting instructional materials, and used as a document to help students, parents and other citizens better understand the purposes and standards used to select instructional materials.

II. GUIDELINES

A. Statement of Policy

The governing body of a school district should declare that it is the policy of the school district to p .de a wide range of instructional materials on all levels of difficulty, with diversity of appeal, and the presentation of different points of view for all students. Further, the governing body should declare it is their policy to allow the systematic review of existing media collections and to permit the reconsideration of allegedly inappropriate instructional materials through established procedures.

B. Statement of Selection Procedures

Responsibility for Selection of Instructional Materials—The governing body of a school district is legally responsible for all matters relating to the operation of the school district. The responsibility for the selection of instructional materials, however, should be delegated to the certificated library/media personnel employed by the school district.

While selection of instructional materials involves many people (library/media specialists, teachers, students, supervisors, administrators, and community persons), the responsibility for coordinating the selection of most instructional materials and making recommendations for acquisition rests with certificated library/media personnel.

The selection of textbooks* may rest with department chairpersons or with textbook evaluation committees.

Acquisition Procedure—A selection procedure should include provisions for the acquisition of all forms of instructional materials. Consistent criteria for selection should be applied to all acquisitions, including gifts, leased materials, and loans.

Criteria for Selection—The school media program is an integral part of the educational program of the school or district. Criteria for the selection of instructional materials should implement this basic purpose.

Instructional materials should be selected on the basis of the: appropriateness of the medium, varying levels of difficulty, student interests, curriculum needs, and representation of varying points of view.

The selection process should provide for the consideration of requests from students, teachers, administrators and the community. Selection of instructional materials should be based upon preview or evaluation reviews in professionally prepared selection aids or other appropriate sources.

Recommendations for acquisition will be solicited from faculty and students.

Gift materials should be judged by the criteria listed in the preceding section and should be accepted or rejected on the basis of those criteria.

It should be understood that selection is an ongoing process which should include the removal of instructional materials no longer appropriate and the replacement of lost and worn materials which are still of educational value.

A media advisory committee following local policy for such appointments may be appointed to assist in the selection and evaluation process.

Procedures for Reconsideration of Challenged Materials—Occasional objections to instructional materials will be made despite the quality of the selection process; therefore, the procedure for handling reconsideration of challenged materials in response to questions concerning their appropriateness should be stated. This procedure should establish the framework for registering a complaint that provides for a hearing with appropriate action while defending the principles of freedom of information, the student's right to access of materials, and the professional responsibility and integrity of the certificated library/media personnel. The principles of intellectual freedom are inherent in the First Amendment of the Constitution of the United States and are expressed in the *Library Bill of Rights*[2] adopted by the Council of the American Library Association in 1948 and amended in 1961 and 1967 and in the *Students' Right to Read*,[3] a publica-

---

* Textbook definition: "any manual of instruction; a book dealing with a definite subject of study systematically arranged, intended for use at a specified level of instruction, and used as a principal source of study material for a given course" (Carter V. Good, ed., *Dictionary of Education* [3d ed.; McGraw-Hill, 1973]).

tion of the National Council of Teachers of English. In the event instructional materials are questioned, the principles of intellectual freedom should be defended rather than the materials.

III. POLICY AND PROCEDURES MODEL

Policy for Selection of Instructional Materials—The _____ School Board hereby declares it is the policy of the _____ District to provide a wide range of instructional materials on all levels of difficulty, with diversity of appeal, and the presentation of different points of view and to allow the review of allegedly inappropriate instructional materials through established procedures.

Objectives of Selection—In order to assure that the school media program is an integral part of the educational program of the school, the following selection objectives are adopted:

- To provide materials that will enrich and support the curriculum and personal needs of the users, taking into consideration their varied interests, abilities, and learning styles;
- To provide materials that will stimulate growth in factual knowledge, literary appreciation, aesthetic values, and ethical standards;
- To provide a background of information which will enable pupils to make intelligent judgments in their daily lives;
- To provide materials on opposing sides of controversial issues so that users may develop under guidance the practice of critical analysis;
- To provide materials which realistically represent our pluralistic society and reflect the contributions made by these groups and individuals to our American heritage;
- To place principle above personal opinion and reason above prejudice in the selection of materials of the highest quality in order to assure a comprehensive media collection appropriate for the users.

Responsibility for Selection—Although the _____ School Board is legally responsible for the operation of the school, the responsibility for the selection of instructional materials is delegated to the certificated library/media personnel.

While selection of materials involves many people, including library/media specialists, teachers, students, supervisors, administrators, and community persons, the responsibility for coordinating and recommending the selection and purchase of instructional materials rests with the certificated library/media personnel. Responsibility for coordinating the selection and purchase of textbooks may rest with appropriate department chairpersons or with textbook evaluation committees.

Criteria for Selection—Educational goals of the local school district, individual student learning modes, teaching styles, curricula needs, faculty and student needs, existing materials and networking arrangements should be considered in developing the media collection. Guidelines for the evaluation and selection of curricula resources are listed.

Curricula materials should:

- Be relevant to today's world;
- Represent artistic, historic, and literary qualities;
- Reflect problems, aspirations, attitudes and ideals of a society;
- Contribute to the objectives of the instructional program;
- Be appropriate to the level of the user;
- Represent differing viewpoints on controversial subjects;
- Provide a stimulus to creativity.

Technical materials should:

- Be of acceptable technical quality; clear narration and sound, synchronized pictures and sound;
- Be readable; typographically well-balanced.

For specific criteria for various forms of materials and equipment, refer to *Media Programs: District and School*, p.70-86.

Procedures for Selection—In selecting materials for school media programs, the certificated library/media personnel in consultation with the selection committee will: evaluate the existing collection; assess curricula needs; examine materials and consult reputable, professionally prepared selection aids. Recommendations for acquisition will be solicited from faculty and students.

Gift materials should be judged by the criteria listed in the preceding section and should be accepted or rejected on the basis of those criteria.

It should be understood that selection is an ongoing process which should include the removal of materials no longer appropriate and the replacement of lost and worn materials still of educational value.

Procedures for Reconsideration of Materials—Occasional objections to instructional materials will be made, despite the quality of the selection process. The _____ School Board supports principles of intellectual freedom inherent in the First Amendment of the Constitution of the United States and expressed in the *Library Bill of Rights* of the American Library Association and *Students' Right to Read* of the National Council of Teachers of English. In the event that materials are questioned, the principles of intellectual freedom, the right to access of materials and the integrity of the certificated library/media personnel must be defended rather than the materials.

If a complaint is made, the following procedures should be followed:
1. Inform the complainant of the selection procedures and make no commitments.
2. Request the complainant to submit a formal "Request for Reconsideration of Instructional Materials" (see Appendix A).
3. Inform the superintendent and other appropriate personnel.
4. Keep challenged materials on the shelves during the reconsideration process.
5. Upon receipt of the completed form, the principal requests review of the challenged material by an ad hoc materials review committee within fifteen working days, and notifies the district media director and superintendent that such review is being done. The review committee is appointed by the principal, with the concurrence and assistance of the certificated library/media personnel, and includes media professionals, representatives from the classroom teachers, one or more parents, and one or more students.
6. The review committee takes the following steps after receiving the challenged materials:
   a. reads, views, or listens to the material in its entirety;
   b. checks general acceptance of the material by reading reviews and consulting recommended lists;
   c. determines the extent to which the material supports the curriculum;
   d. completes the appropriate "Checklist for School Media Advisory Committee's Reconsideration of Instructional Material" (see Appendixes B and C), judging the material for its strength and value as a whole and not in part.
7. Present written recommendation of review committee to the superintendent and the school board.
8. Retain or withdraw challenged materials as mandated by the decision of the school board.
(Appointment of committee members and specific procedures to follow should be made in accordance with local policy. The steps listed above are given as a model to be used in development of local policies and are not suggested as the only procedures which are effective. A procedures policy should include these steps.)

REFERENCES

1. American Association of School Librarians, ALA, and Association for Educational Communications and Technology, *Media Programs: District and School* (Chicago: American Library Assn., 1975), p.1.
2. Council of the American Library Association, *The Library Bill of Rights* (Chicago: American Library Assn., 1967).
3. National Council of Teachers of English, *The Students' Right to Read* (Urbana, Ill.: National Council of Teachers of English, 1972).

IV. APPENDIX A

Request for Reconsideration of Instructional Materials *(Sample)*

School _____

Please check type of material:
( ) Book   ( ) Film   ( ) Record
( ) Periodical   ( ) Filmstrip   ( ) Kit
( ) Pamphlet   ( ) Cassette   ( ) Other

Title _____

Author _____

Publisher or Producer _____

Request initiated by _____

Telephone _____ Address _____

City _____ State _____ Zip _____

The following questions are to be answered after the complainant has read, viewed, or listened to the school library material in its entirety. If sufficient space is not provided, attach additional sheets. (Please sign your name to each additional attachment.)

1. To what in the material do you object? (Please be specific, cite pages, frames in a filmstrip, film sequence, et cetera.)

   _____
   _____
   _____
   _____

2. What do you believe is the theme or purpose of this material?

   _____
   _____
   _____
   _____

3. What do you feel might be the result of a student using this material?

   _____
   _____
   _____
   _____

4. For what age group would you recommend this material?

   _____

5. Is there anything good in this material? Please comment.

   _____
   _____

6. Would you care to recommend other school library material of the same subject and format?

   _____

_____   _____
Signature of Complainant   Date

Please return *completed* form to the school principal.

V. APPENDIX B

Checklist for School Media Advisory Committee's Reconsideration of
Instructional Material—Nonfiction *(Sample)*

Title _____

Author _____

A. Purpose
  1. What is the overall purpose of the material? _____
  _____

  2. Is the purpose accomplished? _____ Yes _____ No.

B. Authenticity
  1. Is the author competent and qualified in the field? _____ Yes _____ No.
  2. What is the reputation and significance of the author and publisher/producer in the field?
  _____

  3. Is the material up-to-date? _____ Yes _____ No.
  4. Are information sources well documented? _____ Yes _____ No.
  5. Are translations and retellings faithful to the original? _____ Yes _____ No.

C. Appropriateness
  1. Does the material promote the educational goals and objectives of the curriculum of
  District Schools? _____ Yes _____ No.
  2. Is it appropriate to the level of instruction intended? _____ Yes _____ No.
  3. Are the illustrations appropriate to the subject and age levels? _____ Yes _____ No.

D. Content
  1. Is the content of this material well presented by providing adequate scope, range, depth and continuity? _____ Yes _____ No.
  2. Does this material present information not otherwise available? _____ Yes _____ No.
  3. Does this material give a new dimension or direction to its subject? _____ Yes _____ No.

E. Reviews
  1. Source of review _____
  Favorably reviewed _____ Unfavorably reviewed _____
  2. Does this title appear in one or more reputable selection aids? _____ Yes _____ No. If answer is yes, please list titles of selection aids.
  _____
  _____

Additional Comments _____
_____
_____

Recommendation by School Media Advisory Committee for Treatment of Challenged Materials
_____
_____
_____
_____

                                        Date _____
Signature of Media Advisory Review Committee
_____   _____
_____   _____
_____   _____

VI. APPENDIX C

Checklist for School Media Advisory Committee's Reconsideration of
Instructional Material—Fiction and Other Literary Forms *(Sample)*

Title _____

Author _____

A. Purpose

1. What is the purpose, theme or message of the material? How well does the author/producer/
composer accomplish this purpose?

_____

_____

_____

_____

2. If the story is fantasy, is it the type that has imaginative appeal and is suitable for children?
_____ Yes _____ No; for young adults? _____ Yes _____ No. If both are marked no,
for what age group would you recommend?

3. Will the reading and/or viewing and/or listening to material result in more compassionate
understanding of human beings? _____ Yes _____ No.

4. Does it offer an opportunity to better understand and appreciate the aspirations, achievements,
and problems of various minority groups? _____ Yes _____ No.

5. Are any questionable elements of the story an integral part of a worthwhile theme or message?
_____ Yes _____ No.

B. Content

1. Does a story about modern times give a realistic picture of life as it is now? _____ Yes
_____ No.

2. Does the story avoid an oversimplified view of life, one which leaves the reader with the general feeling that life is sweet and rosy or ugly and meaningless? _____ Yes _____ No.

3. When factual information is part of the story, is it presented accurately? _____ Yes _____ No.

4. Is prejudicial appeal readily identifiable by the potential reader? _____ Yes _____ No.

5. Are concepts presented appropriate to the ability and maturity of the potential readers?
_____ Yes _____ No.

6. Do characters speak in a language true to the period and section of the country in which
they live? _____ Yes _____ No.

7. Does the material offend in some special way the sensibilities of women or a minority group by
the way it presents either the chief character or any of the minor characters? _____ Yes
_____ No.

8. Is there preoccupation with sex, violence, cruelty, brutality, and aberrant behavior that would
make this material inappropriate for children? _____ Yes _____ No; young adults? _____ Yes
_____ No.

9. If there is use of offensive language, is it appropriate to the purpose of the text for children?
_____ Yes _____ No; for young adults? _____ Yes _____ No.

10. Is the material free from derisive names and epithets that would offend minority groups?
_____ Yes _____ No; children? _____ Yes _____ No; young adults? _____ Yes _____ No.

11. Is the material well written or produced? _____ Yes _____ No.

12. Does the story give a broader understanding of human behavior without stressing differences of
class, race, color, sex, education, religion or philosophy in any adverse way? _____ Yes
_____ No.

13. Does the material make a significant contribution to the history of literature or ideas? _____ Yes
_____ No.

14. Are the illustrations appropriate and in good taste? _____ Yes _____ No.

15. Are the illustrations realistic in relation to the story? _____ Yes _____ No.

Additional Comments

_____
_____
_____
_____
_____
_____

Recommendation by School Media Advisory Committee for Treatment of Challenged Materials

_____
_____
_____
_____
_____

Date_____

Signature of Media Advisory Review Committee

_____   _____
_____   _____
_____   _____

VII. APPENDIX D

American Association of School Librarians Statement on *Library Bill of Rights*

The American Association of School Librarians endorses the *Library Bill of Rights* of the American Library Association.

LIBRARY BILL OF RIGHTS

The council of the American Library Association reaffirms its belief in the following basic policies which should govern the services of all libraries:

1. As a responsibility of library services, books and other library materials selected should be chosen for values of interest, information, and enlightenment of all the people of the community. In no case should library materials be excluded because of the race or nationality or the social, political, or religious views of the authors.
2. Libraries should provide books and other materials presenting all points of view concerning the problems and issues of our times; no library materials should be proscribed or removed from libraries because of partisan or doctrinal disapproval.
3. Censorship should be challenged by libraries in the maintenance of their responsibility to provide public information and enlightenment.
4. Libraries should cooperate with all persons and groups concerned with resisting abridgment of free expression and free access to ideas.
5. The rights of an individual to the use of a library should not be denied or abridged because of his age, race, religion, national origins, or social or political views.
6. As an institution of education for democratic living, the library should welcome the use of its meeting rooms for socially useful and cultural activities and discussion of current public questions. Such meeting places should be available on equal terms to all groups in the community regardless of the beliefs and affiliations of their members, provided that the meetings be open to the public.

Adopted June 18, 1948.

Amended February 2, 1961, and June 27, 1967, by the ALA Council.

These rights are fundamental to the philosophy of school media programs as stated in *Media Programs: District and School,* Chicago, Ill: AASL, AECT, 1975.

Subject Index

Title Index

References in *italic type* indicate illustrations.

Clock Hartley Courseware, Inc. (Apple) 23

CompuPoem Compupoem (Apple) 15

Computer Discovery Science Research Associates (Apple, Atari, TRS-80) 41

Computer Drill & Instruction: Mathematics Science Research Associates (Apple, Atari) 46, 47

Co-PILOT Apple Computer, Inc. (Apple) 30, 44

Crossbow Hayden Book Company, Inc. (PET) 18

Cross Clues Science Research Associates (Apple) 28

Crossword Magic L & S Computerware (Apple, Atari) 46, *47*

Darts Apple Computer, Inc. (Elementary, My Dear Apple) (Apple) 18, 27

Diet Creative Computing (Apple, Atari, PET, TRS-80) 19

Division Skills Milton Bradley (Apple) 23

Ecology Simulations 1 & 2 Creative Computing (Apple, Atari, PET, TRS-80) 17

Engine Apple Computer, Inc. (Apple) 36

Essential Math—Volumes 1 & 2 Radio Shack (TRS-80) 25

Factoring Whole Numbers QED (Quality Educational Designs) (Apple, TRS-80) 19

Fraction-Equiv 1 Microcomputers in Education (PET) 28

Fractions QED (Quality Educational Designs) (Apple, TRS-80) 24

Frog! CURSOR (#19 April 1980) (PET) *14*

Function Grapher Math Software (Apple) 37

Fundamental Punctuation Practice Random House (Apple, TRS-80) 24

Fur Trader Creative Computing (Sensational Simulations) (PET) 16

Furs MECC (American History) (Atari) 16

Galaxy Math Facts Game Random House (Apple, TRS-80) *19*

Game Show Computer-Advanced Ideas, Inc. (Apple) 43, *44*

Geography Explorer USA Instant Software, Inc. (TRS-80) 23

Geography Search McGraw-Hill (Apple, TRS-80) 17, *34*

Geology Search McGraw-Hill (Apple, TRS-80) 36

Geometry and Measurement Drill and Practice Apple Computer, Inc. (Apple) 24

Gertrude's Puzzles The Learning Company (Apple, Atari) 39

Haber (Chemical Equilibrium) CONDUIT (Apple, Atari, TRS-80) 17

Hammurabi Creative Computing (Sensational Simulations) (PET) 38

Hodge Podge Dynacomp, Inc. (Apple) 13

Homonyms in Context Random House (Apple, TRS-80) 27

Ideal Gas Law High Technology, Inc. (Chem Lab Simulations 2) (Apple) 36

Interna-Maze SoftSide (Apple) 19

DATE DUE

Phonics   Science Research Associates (Atari)   *25, 27*

Plot   EduSoft (Apple, Atari, TRS-80)   18

Practicando Espanol Con La Manzana II   CONDUIT (Apple)   20

Problem Solving Edu-Disks   Reader's Digest (Apple, TRS-80)   *39*

Punctuation Skills   Milton Bradley (Apple)   15

Quick Quiz   Radio Shack (TRS-80)   42

Ratrun   CURSOR (#13 August/September 1979) (PET)   19

Readability Analysis Program   Random House (Apple, TRS-80)   46

Reading Level   School CourseWare Journal (September 1981) (Apple, PET, TRS-80)   46

Sammy, the Sea Serpent   Program Design, Inc. (Atari)   *15*

Scatter   CONDUIT (Apple, PET, TRS-80)   36

Scram   Atari (Atari)   *16*

Screen Pro 40   Educational Software Associates (PET)   15

Search   CURSOR (#14 October 1979) (PET)   46

Sell Lemonade   MECC (Apple: Elementary Vol. 3; Atari: The Market Place) (Apple, Atari)   5

Sentence Diagramming   Avant-Garde Creations (Apple)   27

Shell Games   Apple Computer, Inc. (Apple)   42, *43*

Snark   MECC (Apple: Mathematics, Vol.1; Atari: Graphing) (Apple, Atari)   38

Spanish Hangman   George Earl (Apple)   20

Spelling Package   Teaching Tools: Microcomputer Services (Apple, PET)   27

Spell 'N' Time   School CourseWare Journal (September 1980) (Apple, PET, TRS-80)   *27*, 28

Sumer   MECC (Elementary Vol. 6) (Apple)   38

Tag   Creative Computing (Ecology Simulations I) (Apple, Atari, PET, TRS-80)   17, *18*

Three Mile Island   Muse Software (Apple)   16

Titrate   CURSOR (#10 May 1979) (PET)   36, *37*

Touch Typing   Atari (Atari)   16

TRS-80 Color LOGO   Radio Shack (TRS-80)   41

TRS-80 MicroPILOT   Radio Shack (TRS-80)   43

Typing Tutor II   Microsoft (Apple, TRS-80)   24

Voyageur   MECC (Elementary Vol. 6) (Apple)   16

Word Puzzle   CLOAD Magazine Inc. (March 1982) (TRS-80)   46